Nobody Move!
(Without Reading This)

Robert Esposito

Nobody Move!

Copyright © 2024 by Robert Esposito

All rights reserved.

Published by Red Penguin Books

Library of Congress Control Number: 2025927751

ISBN

Print 978-1-63777-647-6

Digital 978-1-63777-645-2

No part of this book may be reproduced in any form or by any electronic or mechanical means, including information storage and retrieval systems, without written permission from the author, except for the use of brief quotations in a book review.

TABLE OF CONTENTS

THE AUTHOR'S NOTE 1
ABOUT THIS BOOK 3
THE PROLOGUE 17

CHAPTER 1: THE ART OF SELECTING A MOVER 29
CHAPTER 2: PACKING 45
CHAPTER 3: BEFORE YOU MOVE: ACTION ITEMS 55
CHAPTER 4: MOVING DAY 67
CHAPTER 5: THE DO'S AND DON'TS OF WORKING WITH MOVERS . 81
QUICK PRELUDE TO TRANSITIONAL SERVICES 94
CHAPTER 6: SELLING ITEMS-ESTATE SALES & ONLINE AUCTIONS . 97
CHAPTER 7: STORAGE 115
CHAPTER 8: CLEAN-OUTS AND JUNK REMOVAL 125
CHAPTER 9: TEMP MOVES (RESTORATION & RENOVATION) 135
CHAPTER 10: MILITARY MOVES 149
CHAPTER 11: BUSINESS MOVES 159
CHAPTER 12: INTERNATIONAL MOVES 171
MOVING THE ELDERLY 185
CHAPTER 14: MOVING PETS 201
CHAPTER 15: DIY MOVES 211

CHAPTER 16: MOVING AUXILIARIES AND ODDITIES 227

CHAPTER 17: MOVING: AN EMOTIONAL JOURNEY................................ 241

CHAPTER 18: THE TRANSITION PEOPLE & PLACES 255

CHAPTER 19: WHAT MAKES YOU HAPPY? 265

ABOUT THE AUTHOR... 275

THE AUTHOR'S FAVORITE POEM 279

THE EXPERTS 280

THE CELEBRITIES WITH EXPERIENCE 280

THE THANK YOU'S 281

THE EPILOGUE.. 283

THE AUTHOR'S NOTE

Transitioning out of a home is one of life's most stressful events. Stress has a way of bringing out the best and the worst in people. So naturally, I was drawn to this magnetic field of high emotions.

From my earliest memory, I had a deep interest in understanding why people do what they do. I was always analyzing people's behaviors and actions. Through my experiences, I have adapted this analysis through different perspectives, based on what stage of life I was in, as well as what stage of life the other person was in. My bachelor's degree is in Human Relations, which prepared me with an understanding of psychology and sociology. I also spent a lot of time studying acting and theology. Prior to starting my moving company, Relocators, my only real job was in the restaurant business. There, too, I learned to read people's behaviors. Examples include the apathy you can see in a couple who are bored with their relationship, or the joy of a family who saved up all month for their one special night at a restaurant. There are tell-tale patterns in human communication, both verbal and nonverbal.

Viktor Frankl, an author, psychologist, and a famous Auschwitz survivor, writes about power in his famous book, *Man's Search for Meaning*: "Between stimulus and response, there is a space. In that space is our power to choose our response. In our response lies our growth and our freedom." When I heard this quote, I immediately related it to a famous scene in my favorite movie, *A Bronx Tale*. A biker gang known for destroying bars comes in to ravage a bar in the mob leader Sonny's neighborhood. When he asks the bikers to leave in a respectful manner, they decline. Instead of running or cowering, Sonny peacefully shuts and locks the front door. As he does, he looks up and says, "Now youse can't leave." That response triggers an immediate deflation of strength and serves as a warning to all the bikers in that bar. What a response!

The dramatic events we face in life are common, although they often feel unique to our own experiences. Responding in a logical way with a proven plan for success often means the difference between success and ease, or failure and problems. The emotion may remain, but moving (pun intended) without emotion can make the difference.

Some of the insights in this book can be found scattered across the internet. But because transitioning out of a home and into a new one can be such a fragmented process, my goal in writing this book is to provide the information all in one place. This will help take an extremely stressful life event—moving—and perhaps make it manageable for you.

My goal for you is twofold. First, hopefully, you'll learn something new through my observations about the human condition, as I have, for the longest time. keenly observed and studied people. I also hope I can help you through any of your transitions relating to this particular topic of moving. I wish for you closure if you're navigating an ending, excitement if an achievement has been met, and most importantly, happiness either way as you approach your new beginning.

Respectfully,
Robert Esposito
The Problem

ABOUT THIS BOOK

"You really wanna get the adrenals going? Leave."
"Nothing, I think, inspires you [more] than taking your house or your history, balling it up…"
—Sylvester Stallone, Sly

ABOUT THIS BOOK

Let this book fill the space and give you power as you respond to whatever transition lies ahead.

Some strategies and themes recur throughout the book by design. Logistical and emotional conundrums intersect here, just as they do in real life.

One of Life's Biggest Stressors

I read a story once about a guy who found out he had terminal lung cancer. The man was from a Mediterranean island but had spent most of his adult life living in suburban New York and Florida. At 66 years of age he found himself unable to work and short of breath.

He went to the doctor and after a series of tests he was diagnosed with terminal lung cancer. He was told he had six months to live.

Although most of his adult life he had spent in America, the man decided to return to his birthplace in the Mediterranean. His reasoning was he did not want to burden his family with the thousands of dollars an American funeral would cost. Rather, he could just go home and be buried beside his family, by the sea. Even though he probably would never see them grow, he wanted to plant grape vines for wine once he got there. He figured his wife could have them as a lasting memory of him. So that is what he did.

I believe we all have this longing for home. The man may have felt at home in America for all of his adult life. Yet when he was confronted with the stark reality of his own approaching death; he decided to go to the place he started. I like that about this story. I also like that it ties death, moving, and serious illness together. In my line of work, I am well aware about how these three life events act together.

Moving is one of life's biggest stressors. According to University Hospitals, it's the third most stressful life event, right after the death of a loved one and divorce. Ranking before major illness or injury may raise an eyebrow or two. Moving is more stressful than cancer? Really? We understand the derisory when we say it in that way.

Consider this. When we think about movers, we usually think of trades, the way we would a contractor, roofer, or deck builder. If anything, our first thought might be a lower-end trade. You know—DIY, rent a U-Haul, that kind of thing. When we plan a move, we are preparing to encounter one of the most stressful life events we'll ever experience. But despite all that stress, we're not seeking out a professional with a degree from some elite university to help us through this rocky time. Instead, we're hiring a bunch of guys with a truck and trusting strangers with our most valuable possessions. In what other scenario does a group of strangers come into your home and remove all of your earthly possessions? I can think of three: criminals, the FBI, and yes, movers.

ABOUT THIS BOOK

We've all had workers in our homes. But usually, these workers aren't handling our most personal things. Your roofer isn't going to accidentally stumble into your most discreet and intimate drawer. Your deck builder isn't touching your family heirlooms. Your handyman isn't sorting through your most sentimental keepsakes from a lost relative. It's an interesting set of dynamics, but that's the moving business. In this field, a little extra care and discretion can go a long way.

That's because our possessions have a strong hold on us as human beings. And that hold can be seen throughout history. In 210–209 BCE, the first emperor of China was buried with a terracotta army, which is believed to be designed to protect him in the afterlife. This practice doesn't end with China. Take the pyramids at Giza in Egypt, built 4,500 years ago. The pharaohs were buried with their most treasured worldly possessions, and sometimes with their living servants, or even living wives and children, to take with them in the afterlife.

So you see, it's human nature to guard our possessions as though they could never be replaced. And when it comes time to move, we are putting a lot of faith in people we barely know to protect our most prized items. Anyone can rent a truck and slap a moving company logo on it. But who is the person driving the truck? I hope it's someone who understands, or at the very least, cares about getting people through some of life's biggest transitions.

Studies show that 7.8% of the US population, or 25.6 million people, moved in 2023.

The Decisions That Must Be Made When Moving

I believe it is important to mention that the stress that we talk about when moving does not just refer to moving day. You will see throughout this book that often, the stress occurs months or years before or after the actual physical execution of a move. Examples of this would be the feelings of empty nests as the last child starts senior year, knowing you're soon going to have to think if the home is too big for your family, all the way through to finding new vendors after a move. As well as everything in between, deciding where to live, buttoning up permits, organizing old attics and hidden spaces, —and then some.

Circumstances of Moving

First, there are all the factors that cause the move—marriage, kids, a new job, death, divorce, downsizing, a home you can no longer afford, and the list goes on.

Maybe one spouse wants to move, and the other does not. The kids do not. The couple is conjoining homes. The couple is breaking up. The siblings are emptying the family home. The family cannot afford what they once could. The family can afford a much better home. The radius you can live in is dictated by a divorce. The radius you need to live in is dictated by wanting to be far enough away from someone.

And then there are the breakups, sparking untold amounts of anger, sadness, or some combination of both. Sometimes people need to move in a hurry before the ex returns. Other times, the way the exes divvy up their possessions is based on spite and revenge. And on top of that, they have to face the actual physical act of moving itself.

Think about the saying, "putting down roots," or making a place your home. I would venture to say that the stress we experience with moving, although it's high on the actual moving day, is really experienced from the inception of the idea that your home will no longer be your home until the move is long past and you feel comfortable in your new routine and start to put down roots.

No matter how organized you are, no matter how much you prepare in advance, moving day can be overwhelming. It's especially true for those with decades of stuff they'd forgotten about but are unwilling to part with, things hidden in dirty, dusty boxes that haven't been touched in years. Maybe they're worth a lot of money, or maybe they hold deep sentimental value—a moment with your now-grown kid, an heirloom from your nana. Who's to say? And now strangers are hauling all of those treasures away. Retaining the kind of mover who knows that the junk box with movie stubs from the first date with a spouse who's passed on is more valuable than your jewelry box can mean the difference between a stressful and a traumatic experience.

There's no doubt that moving is one of life's hardest transitions, and just to get to the other side of it, most people hire multiple providers to get things done. Suddenly, on top of moving, you've got a heap of unexpected expenses. This only adds to the mounting stress.

I feel for everyone in these scenarios. Things happen in life, and people do what they have to do. There are many cases in which the tension only builds. People have to grapple with clean-outs, emergency situations such as fires or floods, estate sales, and storage. I've built my company around providing all of these services based on clients' needs.

The poem, "Reason, Season and a Lifetime" by Brian A. "Drew" Chalker is about the way people come in and out of your life. People always have to move in life, whether for a reason or a season, and sometimes, it's for a lifetime. When you figure out which it is, you'll know better what to do.

The majority, if not all, of the moves that take place in your life will happen under one of the four circumstances below:

The first instance is when your caretaker is making you move because, well, they are your caretaker and they are moving. This move can be simple, like a family moving across town. You often hear people say, "I want to move now before the kids get settled in school."

Next, as you become a young adult, is through achievements and moving through life's stages. You may be going to college, moving for a new job or promotion, moving to the city or the suburbs, getting married, getting a bigger house or downsizing, or retiring.

A little further on can also be through nonachievements in life's stages. (I want to pause to say I chose "nonachievements" instead of "failures" intentionally. What we consider failures differs with each person and is usually based on perception.) These nonachievements could be divorce, loss of job, career change, family reasons, damage, natural disaster, etc.

Then finally it goes full circle and the people you cared for now care for you. Your caretaker is making you move because it is what is best for you. Maybe you're children of adult parents who are moving mom and dad close to home to make sure they have the help they need. Or, maybe you're moving an adult parent into an assisted living facility, a nursing home, to a healthier climate, or perhaps shipping them out on ice floes when they can no longer contribute.

All of these moves come with different struggles and feelings are dredged up during the process. In this book, I want to help ease your stress the best we can. In doing that we want you to know that we understand that the stress that comes with moving is not confined to the move itself. I will show you multiple times that we understand that the stress that comes with moving comes from the moment you are working toward a transition through the actual move and until some special time where your way of life goes back to being settled.

ABOUT THIS BOOK

> *Everything I have done in my professional life has allowed me to observe and experience all of these situations so I can give you the best advice.*

In the early 2000's, my mother started an estate sale company; I will discuss that further ahead in Chapter Six. From my earliest memories, I have been an eternal people watcher. I am, by nature, infinitely curious. In my teens, I carried a video camera, before social media, and tried to write screenplays. In college, I did two years of acting and have an unofficial minor in acting and theology, as well as an official bachelor's degree in human relations, with a focus on psychology and sociology. My only "real jobs" were being a pizza counter boy from ages 14 to 18 and a server/bartender from 18 to 23. Although these jobs were in hospitality and offered the perfect setting for people watching, the latter—Vincent's Clam Bar—taught me valuable skills in business and in human nature.

    I wanted to be successful and in control but I never really had a direct career path or business plan. When I started helping my mother on the weekends with her estate sales, specifically cleaning the houses afterward, I began to see something. Every client was going through unprecedentedly difficult life circumstances and the only solution was a fragmented system of hiring multiple companies. I was done with college, sick of waiting tables, and growing ever so frustrated with wondering what I was going to do with my life.

ACTUAL PAPER FROM THE DAY I INCORPORATED 9/25/08

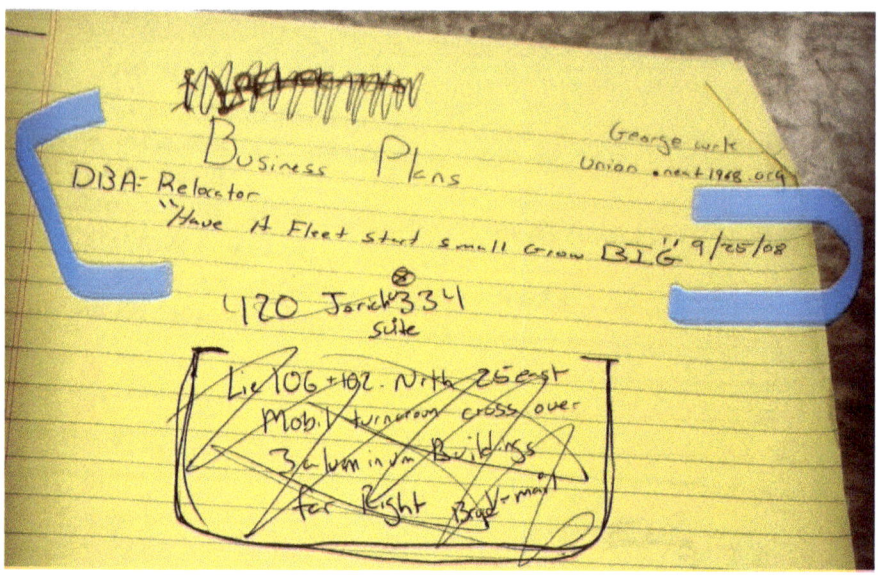

Back in 2008, I scraped together $4,000 to purchase my first box truck and began helping everyone, from those moving into assisted living residences to young couples buying their first homes. Today, my business has over 60 employees and 20 vehicles, along with commercial buildings in two states and thousands of clients who depend on us to help during extremely complicated and stressful home transitions.

With each move, I learned something about the human condition as I stood alongside clients confronting hurdles during some of the hardest times of their life. I helped take away the panic, so life didn't suddenly seem so out of control. I helped them keep their focus so their understandable anxiety would dissipate.

Here in these pages, I share my time-tested tips to help people who are moving. I understand what they are going through because I've been living it since 2007. While I was the one in the background lifting boxes, as an eternal people-watcher, I got to study the human condition.

ABOUT THIS BOOK

As I built my business, I saw it all—from young couples who scraped everything together, eager for a new start, to the captains of industry bitterly tearing up estates.

I also share some moving horror stories at the beginning of every chapter. These are stories from my own experience that I hope you will find engaging. Some can be used as cautionary tales. They also offer some needed levity.

In this book, several themes recur. There are life's big stressors, the ever-present concept that in the moving industry, time is money, and tips about essentials you may need on and around moving day. These essentials include big garbage bags, snacks for energy, and items that keep the kids occupied. In my experience, these helpful reminders will serve to keep you on track as you plan your move.

To this day, I care about the human side of the business of moving. The entire process of transitioning from one home to another involves so many different services. At the end of each chapter I have placed features from experts as well as celebrities who have experiences. Some are directly related to the chapter and others are not. These are placed as an enhancement to strengthen and expand the reader's knowledge beyond just that of moving. In their entirety these tips should help with many of the important processes you will go through as you transition.

Moving is something most of us will have to endure multiple times in life, for both happy and sad reasons. I hope my insights in this guide will help to ease the burdens of moving so people get the fresh new beginning they deserve.

The Prologue
The Chapter Before
No V.I.P.'s in Moving

"Understanding is a three edged sword:
your side, their side, and the truth."
—J. Michael Straczynski

The Story - From An Expert
THE FICKLE FINGER OF FATE
By Dee Snider

I'm a rockstar. Because of that, I usually get special treatment. Which is kinda nice. One of the perks of being famous.

This includes moving. I've never had any problems with my movers who all seem happy to be moving a rockstar, and I've moved a lot.

That's not to say I've never experienced a moving nightmare. I have, but apparently, I was too young (and protected) to be aware of it.

My dad is a Korean War veteran and a former New York State Trooper. He's a tough guy, but for the most part he's a gentleman. While his rockstar son is known for spewing profanity like a drunken sailor (I was even arrested for it in Amarillo, Texas back in 1984), I can count the times I've heard my father curse. Usually it's "ass" (As in, "Stop being a stupid ass!") and on the rarest of occasions "S-H-I-T." He never drops the "F bomb", and I never saw him give someone "The Finger." Living and growing up on Long Island, cursing and flipping someone off is almost obligatory. After all, "Strong Island" is one of the most stressful places in the world to live. If you don't curse, you'll explode. But not my dad.

This said, there is one circumstance when I see my father doing something decidedly ungentlemanly. Any and every time he's driving down Merrick Road through the town of Seaford and he passes a certain long-established moving company, my dad will, almost involuntarily, raise the universal symbol for "eff you" and direct it at said movers. He does it without even turning to look at the place. Once passed, he lowers the offensive digit and continues on.

For a long time, I said nothing about this odd behavior; my dad wasn't the kind of guy you wanted to question, and I worried that he would go from giving it to them to turning it on me.

"You want a piece of this too, smart ass?!" Something like that.

But when I became an adult, and he once again let the "bad finger" fly when passing the moving company, I decided I would finally ask. After all, I am a rockstar. That even impresses my dad.

"So, what's the deal with you giving those movers the finger?" I asked. "What did I do?" he responded.

At first, I thought he was kidding, but I quickly realized he'd been doing this for so long it was just muscle memory. He wasn't consciously aware he was even doing it anymore.

"Yeah, dad. As long as I can remember, whenever you pass that place you flip 'em off."

"You always did have a great memory," he replied.

"And...?"

I wasn't giving up.

"You don't remember what those pieces of shit did to our family when we moved to Florida?" he said, breaking out the rare "s" word, questioning my great memory while starting to get heated.

For the record, I was FOUR years old when we moved to Florida. How much does anybody remember from when they were four?

s the story goes, my dad and his two brothers hatched a get-rich-quick scheme that involved him quitting his job, selling his house in New York, and moving lock, stock, and barrel to the Sunshine State. This was in 1959 long before the mass migration from the North we have down there today. Moving from Long Island to Orlando, Florida was a huge deal, especially for a young family of six. My mother and father were still in their 20's. With four little mouths to feed (I was the oldest), this had to be a pressure cooker of a decision, but they saw opportunity in a pre-Disney World Orlando and decided to roll the dice. The get-rich scheme failed miserably, but that's not what this story is about.

A move of this magnitude couldn't be done with just a box truck and a couple of friends. This required a real moving truck and professionals. So, my father hired the movers who at that time were considered "Long Island's best."

I can only imagine that uprooting his entire family and the massive expense of this move weighed heavily on him. He had to be very aware of every dollar spent and, as a very responsible guy (as responsible as a man chasing a get rich scheme can be), he cut all the corners he could. I remember he sold his prized Lionel train set he'd had since he was a kid, because the size and weight of them made it too costly to move. So away the last vestiges of my father's childhood went.

The day the movers drove away from our Freeport, Long Island home with everything we owned in their professional hands, my parents loaded their four children into our "family truckster" ('You think you hate it now, wait'll you drive it!') and hit the road for Florida. My dad timed the trip so we would arrive at our new house in Orlando before the movers pulled up to unload our belongings.

I do remember arriving at a charming house on a shady block with Spanish moss hanging from the branches of trees lining the street. The air smelled noticeably fresher in Florida back then and my siblings and I ran around the empty house and yard excitedly (those that could, my youngest brother was still in my mother's arms) exploring what would be our new world. Then like clockwork, "Long Island's best movers" pulled up in front of the house with their giant moving van. I remember my dad going out to greet them. And that's when something went wrong. This next part I do not remember, and that's probably because my parents did their best to shield their children so as to not get us upset.

It had taken three long days to get there, and we had driven well over a thousand miles, well before the I-95 had been built. We slowly drove through southern town after southern town, making God knows how many stops along the way (Afterall, we were four small children; "holding it" wasn't our specialty) and now we were waiting in an empty house for our beds, clothes, kitchen stuff and personal belongings so we could start our new lives in Florida. But the movers had other plans.

They claimed my father owed them more money for the move. I don't know for what. I'm not sure my dad even remembers the specifics, but it was complete bullshit and the movers told him they weren't going to unload our things until he paid them a lot more money. This was before credit cards, Venmo, Zelle, or even ATM machines and they wouldn't take a check. They told my dad he had to give them cash or they wouldn't give us our stuff.

Well, my father was a tough guy and didn't put up with this kind of shit from anybody. It was literally robbery as far as he was concerned and he told them there was no way he'd give them a penny more than what was agreed and had already been paid. The mover's response was simple: they would put everything we owned in storage until my dad was ready to give them what they wanted, all the while accruing additional daily storage charges further increasing the amount he owed. My dad looked at his wife and four little children, far from New York, in an empty house with everything we owned about to be driven away…and caved. As much as he hated giving in, he drove into town, went to a bank, and made a cash withdrawal to pay those awful criminals. He gave them the money they demanded, and they unloaded our stuff.

What this moving company had done is a scam as old as movers themselves: tell you one price, load up your worldly possessions, then hold your stuff hostage until you pay more money. And 65 years later this shitty moving company is still in business!?!?

And that's why my 93-year-old dad still gives those effing movers the finger every single time he passes their location. And he lives just one town over! That's a hell of a lot of bad fingers he's thrown at them over the years!

After hearing his tale, and as a family man myself, I understood the frustration my father has with that company to this day. So, now I have taken up his torch and I flip those scumbags the bird every time I pass. And not being the gentleman my dad is, I roll down the window, stick my middle finger out and scream, "EFF YOU!" at the top of my lungs.

That moving company is right across from a police station. Maybe one day I'll get arrested for profanity.

THE ADVICE

That is some story from Dee Snider. I was always a big fan of Dee, from his mega 80's anthems to his resurgence in the 2000's on *The Apprentice* and everything. Also being from Long Island, you often hear about him. My company recently had the opportunity to move his entire family across the country. In getting to know him a little throughout the move I have come to really respect and admire him. There is a lot to unravel here and I totally understand Dee's story. I think most people have heard similar horror stories when it comes to the moving industry.

I want to clear up some misconceptions and provide some clarity of the moving industry from someone who sees both sides of arguments. The company he eludes to may be an entirely different company from the one all those years ago for all I know. I think what happened to Dee's father is terrible. Part of the reason for this book is so many seem to have a similar horror story about a moving company and it impresses how they view the moving industry as a whole. Suffice to say this story depicts the stigma and contention in the moving industry. A microcosm of what we all know exists. Like most industries, moving has its fair share of both great, and unsavory companies. Rightfully so; but in the moving industry things are just much too personal.

Here are some perspectives:

Everyone hears stories of companies holding peoples items hostage until they pay an inflated price. Has this happened, yes. Here is what happens. A moving company is desperate for work and they play the old bait and switch tactic. They low ball an estimate and then after doing half of the job they tell you it is x amount more money, due to whatever xyz reason they give you. They then refuse to unload your life's possessions from their truck until you pay. This is a terrible tactic and has no place in business.

On the other hand, an estimate for a move is just that; an estimate. With moving, estimating is even harder because most times half the job, (the second location) is sight unseen until the truck arrives. Information is power and if a client neglects to tell you certain details then the cost of the job can vary immensely. Important information could be flights of stairs, long walks to the center of a condo complex, freight elevators, narrow driveways that will need a small shuttle truck, smaller second location than first location, and a slew of unknown causes.

Information and communication is so important for accurate estimating. Clients tend to hand pick certain items as not going. Maybe a friend or family member is scheduled to take that piece of furniture. Then come moving day those items need to be moved. I have also had this conversation many times. My foreman will be angry that the estimator is so wrong about the job and now it affects the client's mood during the day as well as his work environment, and possible gratuity.

I know from experience that people try to save as much money as possible until they confirm value. What I mean by that is when a client does not know any better about the level of service, they will tell an estimator things they plan on doing themselves. For instance, they will say no garage, or patio; my husband will do that. Then two hours into the move they say to themselves; wow these guys are great I might as well pay them to do everything. They are happy to pay more, but in the foreman's eyes an eight hour day just turned into 12 hours and now they will end with an angry client and no tip.

Another big issue that often changes the job is packing. Clients say they will be doing the packing and then come moving day they were unable to finish. They either ran out of time, underestimated the workload, or did a subpar job. When movers show up on moving day it is important for the home to be move ready. This means if the client is supposed to be doing the packing, then all items that can fit in a box are already packed and labeled properly.

Additionally, the act of asking for full payment in itself is different for moving than it is for other trades. Circumstances with other trades are mostly solid and the cost is the cost. Your deck builder knows exactly what the cost is and there is little threat to you as the client if he requests most of the payment half way through the job. Your mover however is holding your entire life's possessions. When they ask you for payment there's an inherent hostage perception, which gives you the feeling of being taken advantage of. Couple that with the stigma that there are companies that hold stuff hostage and it makes it even harder.

The scenario in Dee's story does showcase that hostage scenario and it is not ok at all. At Relocators, as well as some other moving companies, we do a lot of things in order to circumvent contentious scenarios.

The Real-World Hacks section below includes the action items I recommend. Each chapter will have hacks, both generalized and specific, to the chapter. Hopefully, these steps will help you as you plan your move.

THE REAL-WORLD HACKS

1. First, we make sure we have clear inventories from the estimate of what is to be moved and what is NOT to be moved.
2. The estimator has a set of questions he must ask to anticipate the logistics and possible issues at the second location prior to doing the estimate.
3. The estimate has a range written in plain site to account for unforeseen circumstances.
4. We take pics of the items and preexisting damage as we enter the home on moving day.

5. We review the estimated scope with the actual scope that the forman has once he does a morning walk through with the client. We discuss and address all inconsistencies and changes immediately.

6. If we do anticipate drastic changes we have a manager from the office call and discuss with the client, the estimator and the on site foreman what their best option is based on their needs and wants.

7. Any changes in job scope are done last, unless addressed by management with the client and a change order is approved. Meaning, if items need repacking or a client adds items, we stop once we complete the estimated job scope and then discuss the added work which will cause added time and added cost. We make sure to manage the expectations in real time and not surprise anyone.

8. Sometimes clients ask to move stuff through areas that really can not be moved. Such as a large sofa through a small hallway. In instances like these we ask the client to sign a best practices release prior to moving that item. At this time, we explain possible risks.

9. When leaving any location we make the client walk through with a foreman and sign a location release. This ensures that nothing is left behind and that it is not the fault of the company if it is.

10. If a client asks to move items around multiple times we make sure they know this uncertainty could lead to higher costs. Being undecided where items go can drastically change the course of a job. Imagine moving every item in a home five times to get it in its right place. This is also why estimates in moving can only be estimates. We make it clear we are here to serve, we will do as much or as little as you like. Just be aware of the pricing structure.

11. The foreman then manages the paths of least resistance in getting the most work done. If there are complicated hallways or rooms we do that last. This way, if time does go over the client can opt to

THE PROLOGUE

leave difficult items in a garage and still have their job completed as planned.

THE CONCLUSION:

I really appreciate Dee's story. It is raw, it is real, and my heart goes out to his father.

A point I like about Dee's story is you will see throughout this book that not the act itself, but everything surrounding moving as a whole is what causes the act of moving to be one of life's most stressful events. A failing business venture, a bunch of young children being displaced, being unsure of needing a future move; all this uncertainty and now this "evil company" is holding your life hostage. I get it. There is an event that takes place that is hard, very hard for everyone involved. The solution is communicating changes from the onset and working together toward a solution for all parties. In this scenario, fifty years of middle fingers turns into fifty years of; "Hey, 23 that's that company we were trapped in a nightmare situation with that really worked with us to find a solution."

> **BONUS TIP:** Moving sucks no matter who you are. Even rockstars can't escape the stress of a move.

THE ART OF SELECTING A MOVER

"Hire a mover who understands that the junk box containing old movie stubs from a first date may be more valuable than your jewelry box."

—Robert Esposito

The Biggest Little City in the World.

Out of state moving is a whole different animal than local moving. There are so many variables and so many logistical obstacles than that of local moving.

With out-of-state moving, the driver is so important. It's hard to hire someone with a CDL (Commercial Drivers License.) You have to birth them, more or less, which means you have to promote drivers and send them to school because for people with CDLs, there's so much work that they can often freelance.

Early on we hired a freelance CDL driver who had his own tractor and trailer. We had a close connection with him because he was a long time employee's stepfather. We had a well-to-do Hamptons client we had moved the year prior and she called to see if we would move her family to California because she was so delighted by the move the year before. My employee had mentioned many times his step father wanted to do out of state trips for us. So when she called I thought this was the perfect opportunity.

Our crew showed up to load the tractor on the load day and I remember being a little taken aback by the appearance of the driver. He seemed rough around the edges; but I dismissed it due to the idea that most over the road truck drivers looked this way. I am someone who relies heavily on gut instincts and I did not feel great. I remember confirming he would take good care of my clients to the point of it almost being OCD. At this point in my life my only truck driver perception was from like the guys Sylvester Stallone arm wrestled in over the top. He fit the bill; minus winning any arm wrestling bouts.

He had one of those personalities that made you walk on eggshells just talking to him. He was respectful toward me but every question was problematic. Either I was asking the world of him or he was reassuring me to the point it seemed phony.

The first few days of the trip went smoothly as he checked in daily and we relayed updates to our client and her family who were now waiting in California for their items to arrive. On day three everything seemed to change. We did not get a check in and in New York we had a very busy day ourselves. I went to bed that night figuring we would hear from him early the next morning and he would be close to their home in California. Last we spoke he was somewhere outside of Reno. Key word here is Reno. After Reno we did not hear from this driver for almost four days. It was a nightmare trying to figure out what was going on. Reno Nevada's slogan is the biggest little city in the world. For those that are not familiar with Reno, I think the best way to describe it is this. After the construction of Las Vegas was complete, the extra debris was dumped in Reno where it formed into a toxic mutated stew of what we now see today.

Every thought imaginable ran through our minds. My employee as well as his mother of all people were calling off the hook. My client was calm but I could tell she was growing more and more concerned by the hour. We wouldn't lie, but we also had no idea; so we just kept playing this guessing game with her for three days.

Finally the third night I got a call from him apologizing. I acted as calm and cool as possible. After all, getting mad would not solve anything—he was 3,000 miles away and there was legitimately nothing

I could do. I asked what's been going on and our client is worried. He responded he had some truck issues and phone issues and in the most nonchalant manner acted like it was all just par for the course. Almost as if nothing had happened. I was baffled by this. I called the client and tried to repeat his candor and assure her the truck would be there in the morning and all was well.

The next morning he showed up at the house and things seemed to make much more sense. The mover we hired in California called to report starting the unload of the truck. We had developed a relationship on the phone the last few days. I asked him how everything looked and to assure me everything was okay with the contents. He said all was good and told me my driver and his wife are exhausted and are going to crash in the cab of the truck while they work. Wife? What wife? I quickly called the driver and in the same nonchalant manner he said oh that's just an old friend from Reno; she wanted to take the ride with me. Everything immediately made sense. At the end of that day the California crew invoiced the client and she was happy with everything. From that moment on I never spoke to the driver again. Of course, I was not surprised a couple years later when my employee told me his mom and step dad were getting a divorce! My one word reply was; Shocking! But I really should have only expended energy for the eyeroll.

THE ADVICE

There's a saying. You can teach people a skill, but you can't teach compassion. Why does this matter when selecting a mover? Because you want to retain someone who can spot what's important to you. Life experiences help develop that instinct, but it starts with empathy.

In my decades of moving people, I've seen things that might seem worthless to the ordinary eye, and yet I knew instinctively that these items were priceless to the client. I'm talking about dated old movie tickets in a bucket on a dresser; maybe they hold a memory of a first date with someone very special. Or an old, faded newspaper clipping; maybe it's a story about something heroic a mother or father was brave enough to do.

The point is that our homes are filled with memories, and your movers should handle them with care. So you'll want to find movers who show respect for the job and take pride in their work. Look for subtle appreciation in the way they interact, both with your belongings and in how they conduct themselves as businesspeople.

Things to Consider When Choosing a Mover

Not all moving companies are created equal. There are a few things to consider that can help you choose the best one. First, look at the moving company's ads. Do they come across as professional? Do you like the platforms that host their ads? What do their ads say about the way they deliver their service?

When you spot their trucks on the road, are they well-maintained? How do their drivers handle the road—aggressively or with safety and consideration for other drivers? A dirty windshield and dashboard in a truck can tell you a lot about a company. All of these factors provide a good indication of what the company is all about.

When you meet with a company representative, are they courteous? Do they take the time to answer your questions? Do their questions show that they're thinking about your needs?

Do you feel a connection when you meet in person? When I first speak with a client, I like to bring in a commonality we might share; maybe my dad grew up in the town they're moving to, or maybe my nana had the same phone when I was growing up. This always resonates with clients because they see I'm taking an interest in them as people, not as business transactions.

Watch to see how responsive a company is. Does the representative return calls right away? Good communication is key because if a challenge surfaces, you want to know that someone is there for you. Subpar communication when purchasing a service is a huge red flag that if something were to go wrong, the communication could be worse.

If the workers are wearing uniforms and are neat in appearance, that shows a level of professionalism in the team and the company that employs them.

As you begin researching companies, look for one that isn't just a financial fit, but is both reputable and trustworthy.

Good vs. Cheap vs. Fast

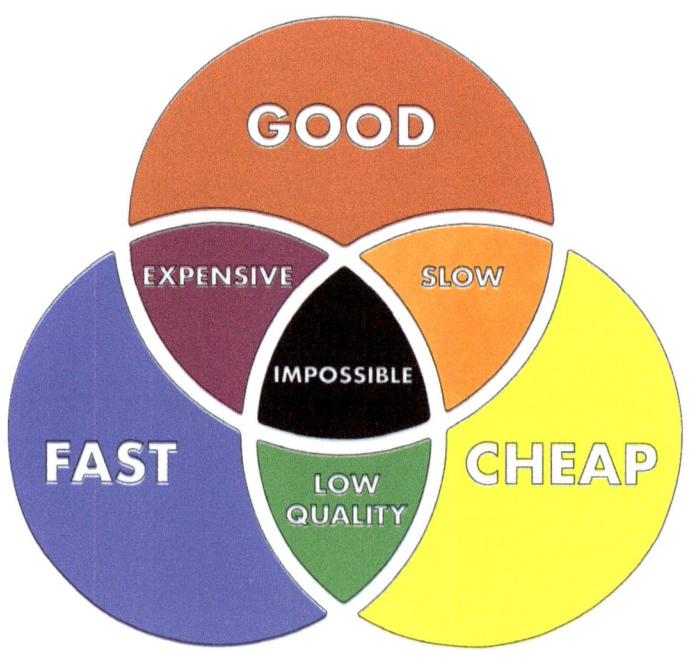

Imagine a Venn diagram with intersecting circles labeled *good, cheap,* and *fast*. In the moving business, you can have two of these, but not all of them. It's possible to get service that is good and fast, good and cheap, or fast and cheap, but the middle—the good, fast, and cheap—doesn't exist. I hear this often: "Do you have anybody who's really good and can be here tomorrow but won't break the bank?" I always think that what they're asking for is a unicorn. It doesn't exist. This is because it's almost an impossibility.

If you have something good and cheap, it's not going to happen soon. You can think about it in moving terms, as an example, where you want the mover's best service and you don't want to pay a lot of money. How can we do that? The best service costs money. If you have 10 boxes that need to go to Florida, and you need it done right away, I can have it done exclusively, it's going to cost you. But if you want to save as much money as possible and you don't have a time frame, I can schedule the pick-up of the boxes next week when we're in your town and then then the next time I have space on a truck, where I just need to add ten extra boxes and the truck is going to Florida anyway, I could do it for you at a really good price. And in that instance, you get good and cheap, but you sacrifice speed.

Secondly, an example of fast and good would be this. Someone calls in and says, "My movers didn't show today. Can you please get us a crew?" Absolutely, we can do this. We have to call people in, the back office has to reroute everything they're doing, we have to get you an ace foreman, get a crew, pull movers from other crews, maybe taxi people around, and all that is added cost. So we're going to get to you quickly and we're going to give you our best service, but you're going to have to cover the extra costs, so it's not going to be cheap.

For cheap and fast, picture a scenario where I don't have the whole back office stop what they're doing and reroute or bring in an ace foreman. What if we sent a message to every crew that's out right at the moment, and the dispatcher sent a foreman and a crew to you. Well, you're going to get a cheaper service, and we'll send it to you quickly, but you're not going to have an ace foreman. We're not going to vet the crew that was sent and it's not going to be our best-quality work. Or, if you rush us during a job and say you don't want crates made or you don't want us to use specific materials that cost more, you'll get cheap work and you'll get fast work, but it's not going to be done with a higher level of quality.

The exception to this rule happens most often in the service business. Restaurants are often an exception to the rule. In restaurants, sometimes you'll get great service, great food, it'll arrive quickly, and you'll get it at an economical price. Vincent's Clam Bar immediately springs to mind. Vincent's is so busy and so successful partly because they've mastered the art of providing a great service or product, at a fast speed, for a very reasonable price. But when you're moving, it can be helpful to first know what's important to you before you start making phone calls. Understanding this is also helpful for reasonably setting your expectations.

The Best Restaurant

THE REAL-WORLD HACKS

1. **Don't let the grass grow under your feet.** Start looking for movers the moment you put your house on the market and check out a minimum of three. The goal should be to settle on the right mover for you by the time you go into contract.

2. **Currency and consistency.** Check their websites. Is everything consistent? Do you see their license number? Is their website current? A dated website can indicate dated business practices.

3. **Invest in the best.** Determine how long they've been in business. If a company is just starting out, it still might be a good fit for you. The key to new companies is to feel very comfortable and have a lot of trust in the operator or owner. Often, they will make up for inexperience with determination. A seasoned mover, on the other hand, could be jaded. With a seasoned mover, you want to know that the person providing your estimate will be available for you when needed. Whether you're talking to the estimator or a moving manager, confirm that you have one point of contact who is invested and committed to seeing your process through.

4. **Comfort zone.** Do they portray themselves in a way that makes you feel comfortable? Remember, you'll be putting your most important possessions in their hands, so trust your gut.

5. **The devil is in the details.** Read the reviews, which are so important. Do the reviews seem authentic? You'll want to hire a mover that has lots of reviews, and whose reviews don't sound like they were all written by the same person. Dig into the details and see how the company replies to comments. For example, is someone responding professionally to both the positive and negative reviews? Do those reviews and comments paint a story and provide insight into the company, or are you seeing only generic five-star reviews

that reveal nothing about a customer's experience? Don't let some negative reviews discourage you from choosing a mover; better yet, study them practically to see if they are warranted and how well the company is accountable to them.

6. **Twenty questions.** Ask questions but think first about the kind of information you're seeking, and why. For example, some people ask if my crews speak English, and it seems at times that they are dancing around prejudice. Of course, you want to be able to communicate well, but equally important is retaining a hard-working, nimble crew from a culture that cares, no matter what language they speak. These are the people who work at Relocators and they have always done right by the company and our clients.

7. **Legal equals secure.** Choosing a licensed moving company is important. Sure, the unlicensed movers may charge half the price, but without the proper certificates, there is nothing to regulate, and families put themselves at risk with no legal recourse.

8. **Plan for the best; prepare for the worst.** Make sure you understand insurance valuation. If you're considering homeowner's or renter's insurance, get a firm grasp of what is covered. Valuation is complicated and your move is probably not insured the way you think it is. Different states have different policies. Your best bet is to research your state's policies. Thoroughly ask about and read all the information your estimator gives you. Insure yourself through homeowner's and renter's insurance when possible. Some homeowner and renter policies allow for a rider to cover contents for a specific time frame. This is a great option that you should ask your broker about if it is available.

9. **Be specific.** Moving charges are often based on hourly rates, so communicate clearly what you are going to move, as well as the logistics at both locations.

THE ART OF SELECTING A MOVER

10. **Save smart.** When meeting with the estimator, be sure to plan the move properly. It's common for homeowners to say they will move 50% of their items to lower the moving costs. Their immediate thought is to do things like tackle the miscellaneous items in the garage or relocate the outdoor furniture or boxes on their own. The irony is that, because the cost of moving is based on time, the 50% of items they moved may only account for 10% of the actual time and cost of the total move. Doing intricate things like removing TVs from the wall or disassembling furniture will save you a lot more in moving costs. The movers will be able to pack up the above-mentioned garage and the boxes extremely fast—it's the kind of work they do every day, and they have it down to a science. Rather than focusing on 50% of the content, focus on the tasks that would entail 50% of the moving time to reduce your costs. Dismounting TVs and fragile items, along with dismantling furniture and equipment, are the most time-consuming, even if these materials only account for 10% of the items being moved. They may actually account for much more of the move time, which, in turn, accounts for money.

11. **Nothing is certain but change.** If you sign on with a mover, make sure you understand the cancellation policy. People may need to cancel if the lawyers are still working through legalities the day before closing, and the other homeowners may have issues. This is more common than you might think. I've seen people change their move date five to 10 times. Understand what the cancellation penalty would be, if any, before you hire a moving company. There shouldn't be a penalty for changing the dates, because anyone in the industry should understand that the client will use the moving company and that if something happens with the closing, it's out of the client's control.

THE CONCLUSION

You can see from the horror story that hiring the wrong mover can cause unprecedented amounts of stress. A lot goes into hiring a mover and it should not be taken lightly. Knowing your needs and wants is crucial to making the right decision of what works best for you. Make sure to request on site estimates and take your time disclosing as much pertinent information as possible for both locations. Virtual estimates and pictures sent over also work well for estimates. Again the onus is on you and you may be prone to leaving things out that you would not if the estimate were in person. So with virtuals and pictures be conscious of the details even more. When comparing estimates make sure to compare apples to apples and look to compare men/time over money. You always want to understand what the service is, and that multiple estimators are agreeing on your needs. The price for that service can be analyzed after you have determined that the service needed is consistently agreed upon.

Up next: packing and all the thrills of digging into dark corners and crevices of your home.

> **BONUS TIP:** When selling your residence, make sure your real estate attorney gives you a 72-hour grace period for moving out of your home. That way, in the event of some unexpected delay, you avoid unnecessary financial penalties. *(Note - Some states may not require attorneys, regardless when possible look for a grace period.)

THE EXPERT

Matthew Rivera: Insights from the Founder of Inspection Boys

Matthew Rivera isn't just a home inspector; he's a real estate enthusiast who wears many hats. As the founder of Inspection Boys Franchising, owner of a home inspection school, and a house flipper, Matt has a wealth of experience in all things real estate. Having seen and heard it all, his unique perspective offers invaluable insights into the home-buying process. Here are a few of his tips and some stories from the field:

Be Present in the Home-Buying Process

One of the most critical tips Matt offers is to be actively involved in the home-buying process. It's easy to take things lightly, but remember, from the agent to the lawyer, title company, home inspector, and moving company, the choice is yours. Recommendations are helpful, but ultimately, you are in control. If you don't like someone, hire someone else. Once you buy the house, all problems become yours.

Case in Point: *I once had a client who spent a Saturday viewing 10 houses and made offers on three. By Sunday, they had an accepted offer and needed to be in contract by Tuesday. In their rush, they scheduled a home inspection for Monday. Initially, they didn't plan to attend, but their agent insisted. When they arrived, they were ready to pay and leave, convinced the house was perfect. I pointed out that the listing described a three-bedroom house, yet they believed it was four. After a heated discussion with the agent, it turned out they had bid on the wrong house. If they hadn't attended the inspection, they would have signed contracts for a house that didn't meet their needs.*

Just Because it Works Doesn't Mean it's Fixable

Many homeowners, especially engineers, like to experiment with their homes, modifying systems like boilers or pool pumps. While these custom solutions may work for them, they often create problems for future owners. If something breaks, only the original tinkerer can fix it, making repairs more expensive and complicated for you.

Expect Things to Break

Whether the house is brand new or decades old, things will break. It's a part of homeownership. It's easy to blame everyone involved in the process when something goes wrong, but understand that maintenance and repairs are inevitable. Embrace the challenges of owning a home and be prepared for unexpected issues.

Final Thoughts

Homeownership is a rewarding journey, but it requires attention, involvement, and preparedness. By following these tips and staying engaged in the process, you can avoid common pitfalls and make informed decisions.

PACKING 2

"Everyone seems to have a clear idea of how other people should lead their lives, but none about his or her own."

—Paulo Coelho, The Alchemist

DIVORCE CADABRA

One client we moved was going into storage prior to moving with his whole family down to Florida. Originally, I remember his whole family seemed happy on the estimate and excited to be moving to Florida. First, he was coming into storage for 6 months to one year while he found a dream home for his family in Florida. He negotiated hard for a special deal since he was packaging two moves and storage altogether. This was early into my career, I was still wet behind the ears and succumbed to his negotiations by giving him six months free storage. I made a total rookie mistake by making such a bad deal. The silver lining was a move to Florida at this time was a very big deal for me. What I did not know was this deal was going to prove to be much worse than I could have ever imagined. I turned out to be just another pawn in his scheming plan.

The furniture ended up staying in storage for six years without one cent being paid the entire time. You see, instead of dealing with all the grown up responsibilities and uncomfortable situations that come with a divorce; this client hatched a pretty malicious yet ingenious plan. He told the whole family they were moving to Florida. Really he was just waiting to break the news that he was divorcing his wife. Right after he moved it into storage, he left his wife and we immediately started getting calls from her to come get some of her possessions. Then letters started coming from courts and divorce lawyers of her fighting for her stuff in court. We were both victims in this mess but we could not help each other because the courts sent letters about freezing the contents until all was settled. There were court orders that no one could touch anything or be allowed to see their property.

Could you imagine having three young children and putting 90% of your young children's possessions in temporary storage and not touching it again until your children are teenagers. I know there are two sides to every story but no parent should allow their children to be collateral damage, ever.

This was not a normal storage situation where we could auction off delinquent contents. First, we felt bad for this woman who was a victim in all of this. Second, the courts clearly asserted that nothing be touched until a resolution was made.

Six years passed and finally it was determined that the couple's divorce would be settled. The couple, or ex couple, split the entire storage bill and the next day the woman hired us to deliver her items to her new home in Florida. I remember thinking good for her. She followed the plan without him.

The woman and myself were two victims of the same event. In the end, I got paid most of the money, but it was a nightmare for years. Imagine your husband moving your entire household into storage because you think you're starting a new life in a new home that you're custom building in Florida with your family. Then, as soon as all your belongings are in storage, your spouse pivots the other way and you have to fight for your things in court for four to five years.

THE ADVICE

Packing is a chore, no doubt, but when people finally get around to packing up their stuff, they usually have two goals. They want to protect their treasured items and they want to save money. Let's face it—moving is expensive.

A lot of emotion is tied to our belongings. The value of our things often depends on the people and memories we associate with them. Boxes of family photos, objects passed down through the generations… these things mean a lot to us and they are irreplaceable. Handling them with special care is important to ensure they endure the move intact.

Sentimental and valuable items—jewelry, medals, heirlooms, and any other precious objects—should be packed and stored in a separate room or partitioned-off area. On moving day, they should be locked in a vehicle to keep them separate from the rest of the items and to make them easy to locate. These items should be moved personally and not by a company.

If financial savings is your goal, you can reduce costs by doing a lot of the packing yourself—especially if you are strategic. Packing your items yourself can be a significant cost-saver, as retaining a packing service can double the cost of a move, in some cases.

One thing to consider is that most moving companies will not cover items packed by the homeowner. On inventory sheets you will see this marked as PBO (packed by owner). So make sure items not professionally packed are still packed in a professional manner. Broken items will cause the savings you retained from packing yourself to be fruitless.

Others, who feel confident in their movers, may have them pack the items and point out what is of special importance. I always recommend checking around the home, under beds, in the basement, and anywhere precious items have been tucked away. Doing this before the movers arrive will help ensure there are no surprises, and hopefully, no last-minute reasons to scramble on moving day.

THE REAL-WORLD HACKS

1. **Wrap it with kid gloves.** Plan your advance packing wisely by doing the things that take the most time first. Start with your least-used nonessential items, and remember to wrap intricate, fragile items. Don't forget to remove wall hangings.

2. **Purchase packing materials wisely**. Typically, home improvement stores and online vendors will have the least pricey materials, while storage facilities and office supply stores tend to be more costly. Skip the bubble wrap, which is expensive, and opt for newsprint, which is like newspaper without the print on it, when crumpled, provides good air cushioning for items. Wrap each piece in at least one individual sheet of paper.

3. **Time is of the essence.** Begin packing as soon as possible. If you don't have a tight time limit, you can pace yourself by doing a little at a time and be completely packed by moving day.

4. **Time saved is money earned.** Agree with any significant others who will be living with you about your new layout in advance. Predetermine where you want movers to bring items, rather than fussing with furniture layouts on moving day. The more time you spend on room arrangements on moving day, the more it will cost you. With an agreed-upon layout, label boxes accordingly, specifying the room, the contents, and the floor. For example: (Kitchen, Dishes, 1st Floor). This saves time because you don't have to tell the movers where every single item goes. Time is money.

PACKING

5. **Bottoms up.** Always pack heavy items on the bottom of boxes and layer lighter items on top to fill the boxes.

6. **Sometimes labels are a good thing.** Have empty boxes ready and labeled for last-minute things such as remotes, TV cables, electronics accessories, toiletries, and similar items.

7. **Filler items.** Pack inexpensive throw pillows and blankets in heavy-duty construction bags. These bags are cheaper, and soft items provide good space-fillers in the truck that protect other things while the truck is moving.

8. **Smart arrangements.** Are there specialty items to pack? Consult with your mover on anything that's fragile or special. Ask who should pack the items and which materials to use. Label these items clearly. Your mover should have extensive knowledge of where on the truck fragile packed items should go. Some items are safest in the "grandma's attic," the small space over the truck's cab. Other items are best situated on the top of a tier towards the cab, while others like perishable food, and plants, should be last in and first out. Specifically discuss the fragile items with your movers to help ensure their safety and that they place them in the proper places when packing the truck.

9. **Photograph it.** If you do not plan on unpacking all items right away, it's a good idea to take pictures of the contents of each box. This is easy to do while packing and could be a huge time-saver if you need to look for anything later. Place the box on a table, then place all items you plan on putting in that box next to it. Put a number or a numbered sticker on said box and snap a picture of the box with the contents next to it.

10. **Small packages.** Heavy items like books should be packed in smaller boxes. Making large boxes too heavy will make them clunky and hard to carry.

11. **To pack or not to pack.** Here is a great rule of thumb to differentiate between wrapping and packing. Anything that fits in a large box or smaller is considered packing and anything larger is part of the items that need to be wrapped. Wrapping of items should be included as a standard as part of your move service.

12. **The Re boxes.** Re-Fuel, Re-Member me, Re-Charge, Re-Fresh; are specific boxes we use at Relocators to differentiate some important items for our clients. Re-fuel, is for snacks and medicines on moving day, especially for kids, young children, and elderly. Re-member me, are all the important papers and documents that you want to make sure do not get lost or misplaced. Re-charge, is all the remotes, wires, charges, etc. Re-fresh, have all your needed toiletries at the new home in one specific box.

THE CONCLUSION

I chose the horror story for this chapter opening because I wanted to highlight a very important item I briefly mentioned. Now, I know this story is far fetched and likely will not happen to most people; I hope! The concept that you can pack something and not have it when you need it due to an unforeseen event is very common with moving. Make sure nothing of urgent importance or need is packed and sent with the mover. Things like medicine, jewelry, power cords, are among some of the important items that you should have separated when the movers arrive and make sure you take them yourself. I think a good rule of thumb for packing is this. Anything you would need on an extended vacation or long getaway should be kept with you and never packed onto a truck, or in storage. This baseline will give you some protection from the happenstance of an extreme situation.

PACKING

Next, we will talk about last minute action items just before the actual move.

> **BONUS TIP:** Reinforce heavy boxes with extra tape at the bottom to prevent contents spilling out during transport and avoid making boxes too heavy. Heavier items can be distributed among boxes with lighter items packed on top. Boxes should be constructed with flaps intertwining prior to taping to create a more secure bottom and top. (This references boxes with four flaps at the top and four flaps at the bottom.) When you fold the four flaps on the bottom, each flap should have one side under the adjacent flap and one side over its other adjacent flap. This will hold the box together in a stronger way.

THE EXPERT
Steven E. Shumer, Matrimonial Expert

With moving being one of the most stressful situations a person can face, compounding that with a move as the result of a divorce can often be unbearable. To protect yourself and ease the stress of a move after divorce, we recommend the following:

As soon as the divorce process commences, take photos and videos of the entire house and its contents. In a contentious situation, there will almost always be a claim that one party or the other removed or is hiding property; the photos and videos can add some level of protection. Create a written inventory of all jewelry of concern. Take photos of the jewelry. Then, on notice to the attorneys and both parties, place all jewelry in a safe deposit box until the distribution is agreed upon.

Provide your attorney with a detailed list of the important and/or valuable pieces of property that you feel have to be addressed in the context of the divorce negotiations. This could be a valuable piece of art, photographs and videos, or family heirlooms. "Value" is not established by a monetary worth; "value" is set by each person and their connection to the property.

When removing property from a home after a settlement or judgment, have a third-party witness present from each side to assure that there are no claims that either party took items to which they were not entitled.

Remember, any piece of property can be removed from a home, with either party claiming they never saw it, removed it, or maybe even that it was never even owned. Even with a paid receipt, there would be no way of proving that one person or the other took possession or removed a specific piece of personal property. Inventorying the items and documenting everything is vitally important to securing your rights so that the removal and moving of property after the divorce settlement proceeds with ease and without conflict.

BEFORE YOU MOVE: ACTION ITEMS

"By failing to prepare, you are preparing to fail."
—Benjamin Franklin

REAL STAKES

Once, a real estate lawyer called me when a real estate deal was falling through. The moving company had walked away. If the client, a hoarder, wasn't out of the house by Sunday night, the buyer, the Realtor™, and the real estate lawyer would lose the deal. The house would go into foreclosure on what was probably a $600,000 to $800,000 sale. We did an in-home estimate that same day for $12,000 based on what the homeowner said she was taking. We photographed and inventoried everything she wanted to take, which was a tenth of what was in the house.

We knew there were red flags all over it but we wanted to do the work for the real estate lawyer. The last moving company had quoted the client a cost of $12,000 or $13,000 and then later, told her it would be $20,000. After the second day of the job, she had paid half of our bill and it was easily going to $20,000 and beyond. She was trying to keep everything. The packing and moving process for a hoarder means ten times the work. Reality clashes with must have needs that are really misconstrued wants. Hoarders tend to sway back and forth with decisions and are extremely impulsive with decisions. It is like their mind lives at the corner where analysis paralysis meets addictive depression. Figure that out.

We updated her on the estimate as it went. We also continued to tell her that every place she was pointing was not what we have in the estimated inventory. She continuously said, whatever it costs; I have to take those items. We gave her different releases for each change and my foreman was smart. Not only did he have her sign the releases, he also filmed her signing them.

Finally, Sunday she said we were done because she said she reached her spending limit and would just take what is already in the trucks.

She also did not know when she could move into her new house. That came out of nowhere. We were completely led to believe the entire weekend that this was going to be a direct move. So basically the woman who could not pay for her move now was almost doubling it by asking for storage indefinitely.

A friend of hers called me a couple weeks later asking for her stuff. The friend seemed unhappy and a bit aggressive. He mentioned some items about the move and I quickly explained that he was very confused. He was under the impression that we refused to take her stuff and then kept what we did take hostage in storage. I explained to him she sent it to storage and the rest of the situation. His demeanor quickly turned. I offered to set up the move immediately. He was so appreciative he offered to cover her incidental move balance the day of the unload.

Six months later, I was served with a lawsuit of $120,000. It was the only time I have ever been sued for anything. She tried to say that we forced her to leave her treasured items in her house. I sent my lawyer the signed releases, a video of her signing them, and a video of her saying what a great job we did and that we took everything she wanted. The case was thrown out for $0. I think I paid my lawyer about $400.

THE ADVICE

All the Planning in the World

Tom ended the call, smiling. He'd lined up all the details necessary to organize a double closing. He even allowed for several hours in between the closings, so that in one day, he would sell his current home, take ownership of his second location, and move out of the old home and into the new. The house would be packed up by noon, and the boxes and furniture unloaded by 3 p.m. This required a lot of planning, but Tom managed to schedule all of it with some time to spare.

What Tom didn't realize, despite all of his intricate arrangements, was how fast a move can get derailed. Maybe the financing falls through. Or there's a problem with the paperwork, or perhaps, an unanticipated issue with the final walk-through.

Any one of these matters, as well as an infinite number of others, can cause a delay or cancellation of the closing. And to make matters worse, should Tom's plans backfire on double-closing/moving day, he might have movers who showed up at the house at 8 a.m. to get a jump start on packing it up. Where would Tom and his family wind up going? And what would happen to all their stuff?

Talk about stress. It's like running a marathon and adding a 25-pound weight at an incline. Maybe you remember the scene in *Apollo 13*, when, after the command service module was no longer functioning, the astronauts realized they needed the lunar module to stay alive and get back to Earth. In the film, Fred Haise says of the lunar module, "She wasn't designed to fly attached like this. Our center of gravity is the command module." And Jim Lovell agrees, saying, "It's like flying with a dead elephant on our back." And to make matters worse, the moving costs are now escalating, with unexpected storage fees and maybe even a night or two at a hotel, meals out, and the list goes on.

Unfortunately, there are many people like Tom who find themselves in this exact kind of predicament when moving. This is why, in the Chapter 1 Bonus Tip, I mention having a real estate attorney build in a three-day grace period for moving out of your home. It's also why I always work with clients to help them avoid the unexpected and keep the move as stress-free as possible.

THE REAL-WORLD HACKS

1. **Plan to be delayed.** Make sure you work with your attorney in advance to add a buffer for unforeseen delays that might hinder the moving schedule.

2. **Left behind.** Mark all items that are to be left in your old home for the new homeowner. Label them prominently, so the movers do not mistakenly put them on the truck.

3. **Prepare to transition.** Determine when the house needs to be empty for the walk-through and when it should be ready for the new owners.

4. **Save the date.** Know the first date and time you can be in your new location.

5. **Time after time.** Ask your mover the estimated number of hours it will take to load your items before they leave for the second location, as well as the unloading time. This could prove to be invaluable in helping you to plan and prepare. Note that the times are just estimates, so avoid planning in a way that would constrain the schedule.

6. **Make a reservation.** If you're moving in or out of an apartment building, does an elevator need to be reserved, and if so, what is your time window? Does your building need a Certificate of Insurance

BEFORE YOU MOVE: ACTION ITEMS

(COI) and is it approved? Ask your building super or management company prior to moving day and know the rules. Apartment buildings, for example, may have specific rules and regulations that limit when people can move in and out. Get those policies in advance and plan accordingly.

7. **Size matters.** How big of a truck does your mover anticipate you will need? What happens if you wind up taking more items than you thought you would? You'll want to plan all of this in advance, as your mover calculates the number of cubic feet required for your move. Find out what ratio you need compared to the cubic feet of the truck and the estimated cubic feet to move your items. If it's within a 20% variance, ask your mover if they have a backup plan if there's not enough room on the truck.

8. **Plan for a smooth handoff.** Ensure someone will be at the second location to guide the movers as they unload the truck so they know what goes where in the new home.

9. **The lay of the land.** Does either location present challenges that might complicate the move? Narrow driveways, far walks from the curb to the home, small elevators, and more can become problematic. By anticipating these things in advance, you'll get the most accurate estimate, and equally importantly, reduce stress.

10. **Before, during, and after.** Set clear expectations of when you want the move to be finished and ask your movers about options. Consider the possible time frames. Are you open to one long, 16-hour day, or do you prefer two 8-to-10-hour days? If the second location is a distance away, some people like to do a prep day, a load day, and an unloading day, and arrange for a place to sleep on the second and third days. A prep day is prior to the move day, and in most cases, a day or two before.

On this day, the movers wrap and disassemble all the nonessential items and take their time packing or wrapping the fragile items. In the instance when a move is a short distance, you might do a prep and load day, keep a bag of essential items at hand, and then unload first thing the next morning for a quick moving day. Different expenses are involved with each arrangement. Consider not only the financial but also the emotional costs, and which option provides the most value to your family.

11. **Security.** If your move will take more than one day, ask where your items will be stored. Will the movers store your belongings in a locked yard with security cameras? If the movers are sleeping at a motel, how will the truck be protected?

12. **End-to-end planning.** In the event of a long-distance move, who will be on the other end? While most movers might retain a third-party to assist with the haul, it's best if one or two from the first location are there to complete the move.

13. **The Relo Ree's.** Re-member me; all your important items and paperwork in a specific box. Re-fuel; all your quick snacks & drinks in a cooler or small box. Re-charge; all your charging cords and kids devices in a specific box. Re-fresh; all your needed toiletries at the new home in one specific box.

14. **Services Set.** Make sure all utilities and services such as locksmiths are scheduled and accessible as you need them. Call and plan in advance to find out schedules and time frames.

15. **Set up and settle up.** Set up your utilities for your new home one to two weeks in advance. Plan to return any utility equipment, like routers, and settle the accounts for your old residence.

THE CONCLUSION

Preparedness is crucial prior to moving day. As a company our biggest red flag about a client is when someone calls last minute for a move. You know right away that the complications will be exaggerated because a move is rarely some emergency last minute event. Hack number 13 alone will save a lot of headaches on moving day by having essential things handy instead of having to search for them. I would argue that the amount you prepare prior to moving day is in direct correlation with the ease and smoothness you will experience the day of your actual move. During your last confirmation with the moving company make sure to get the foreman or operation manager, or dispatchers number. You want to be specific about having a number for someone who will be accessible before office hours in case you need to contact them early on moving day morning. People are often inclined to have people come see their new homes as they are moving in. Although not optimal, this is ok; I strongly recommend not being stuck to any plans or dinner arrangements. If someone wants to stop by it's better they stop by to help rather than hinder.

Prepping complete; here comes the big day–moving day up next.

BONUS TIP: Before selling your home, make sure there are no open permits from previous years that could impede the sale. You may even want to go to your town hall and ensure everything is satisfactory. Often, it's an open permit on a shed or a basement that can put a sale in jeopardy.

BEFORE YOU MOVE: ACTION ITEMS

THE EXPERT
James Garvey, Mortgage Expert and Loan Officer

Securing mortgage financing when moving to a new home or renovating your current residence involves several important steps and considerations to ensure a smooth process. By carefully preparing and understanding the mortgage process, you can navigate your move to a new home or refinance more effectively.

Similar to choosing the right relocations specialist, it's crucial to select a true mortgage expert who has the expertise and professional track record in serving your best interests, and providing various options that are cost-effective. A trusted mortgage expert will be equipped to assess your credit and financial situation, determine your budget, and guide you through the pre-approval process when buying a home, or qualifying your ability to access your home's available equity when refinancing.

If you are looking to purchase a home, a certified pre-approval that verifies your buying power will need to be in-hand when looking at homes that are on the market. A pre-approval letter that is signed by a well-known mortgage professional strengthens your position as a buyer and will separate you from the other prospective buyers out in the market.

When refinancing your current mortgage to fund a renovation, it's crucial to know which financing options are the best fit for you. Whether an extensive renovation is requiring a temporary relocation, or you want to embark on a relatively minor project, there are tailored products and programs available that will need to be analyzed from a cost and flexibility perspective.

Regardless if you're purchasing or refinancing, a key tip to be mindful of is current housing market conditions. Research the local market to understand property values and trends with a trusted real estate agent. Be prepared for competitive markets where offers over the asking price might be necessary, or other solutions your lender can suggest you leverage. Some markets yield the buyer to negotiate on their behalf and save some of their hard-earned funds for costs like furniture and movers.

This information was provided by James Garvey, a top-performing mortgage expert and loan officer with over 20 years of mortgage lending expertise in all 50 states. In addition to assisting clients directly, James leads his own mortgage lender branch on Long Island, New York, where he manages a top-performing group of loan officers who also assist their own clients with mortgage solutions. Both James and his branch hold various, multi-year customer service and performance awards, and consistently rank in the top three branches in the region, and the top 10 branches nationwide, as of 2024. NMLS # 314551

James' client profiles include first-time home buyers, relocation and move-up buyers, estate/divorce buyouts, and high-net-worth borrowers. Lending areas of expertise include conventional, non-conventional, jumbo, state, government (FHA, VA, USDA), and affordability lending. Additionally, James holds various certifications, including new construction, renovation, and wealth lending. All mortgage financing inquiries welcomed at jamespgarvey.com.

MOVING DAY 4

"All things change; make peace with what's ending and welcome your new beginning."
—Robert Esposito

Spite revenge, tomato-tomahto

One client on moving day was understandably furious. In a divorce settlement, he'd lost the family home that his parents had owned for 100 years. What had started out as a bungalow was now a sprawling house that he had expanded with multiple extensions over time. What I loved about it was that you could literally guess exactly when he did each extension. Each section reflected the decade of the new extension. The nineties extension was all glass and windows. The eighties extension was filled with mirrors that were popular at the time. The seventies section had wall to wall movie screens and shag carpeting. Now, the woman he'd been married to for 30 years was getting the house. The house was a hodge podge stylewise but it was unique and had character. You could walk the decades from room to room and that was pretty cool.

I had done two or three estimates for him already. But on moving day, the client said, "This is my family's house. Can you believe this? As of yesterday she got the house, but I'm getting all the contents." I remember his gaze as he adamantly stamped out the words, "I will show her." I was puzzled for a second and then soon realized what he meant. It meant that we were in for it. And with that, a two-day move turned into an eight-day move. He took everything, making us unskillfully remove—the cabinets, the toilets, the sinks. Anything that could be removed he had us remove. As we rolled up the carpet the feeling of never being free of this job came over me. I mean the carpets and padding; I am not talking about throw rugs. Money was no object to him. Need for items or waste also had no effect on him. Everything pales in comparison to his desire to make sure that house she owned had zero inside of it.

"I can't believe this is real life," was the phrase you heard every single time a worker unloaded an item at the truck.

The client was eccentric to begin with. He was like the results of Doc from Back to the Future having a baby with the homeless pigeon lady in Home Alone 2. Pour on some psychedelics. He owned a building with a domed skate rink that he had constructed in the side lot. He had us move everything to that rink and reconstruct it in a similar manner to how he had it in his home. He took the emotion of moving to a level I had never seen. With any issues with financials out of the way we prided ourselves on doing as much or as little as our client asked of us. So we just kept working. I wanted so badly to see her face when she walked into that house and saw what he did. I was sure she would be shocked until Julio, my foreman, brought up a fabulous point. "No, she divorced him after 30 years, she knows what she's gonna get."

THE ADVICE

Google life's biggest stressors, and you'll come up with death, divorce, and moving; combine two of the three of life's top stressors, and you're bound to have some stories of your own.

On moving day, don't be surprised if you're flooded with emotions. You may suddenly feel uncertain about even the smallest decisions. Or sad. Or angry. And you are sorting through all of it—and maybe also dealing with your life partner, and perhaps the rest of your family's needs—all while a bunch of guys are loading and unloading a truck with all of your belongings.

Take a breath. You'll get through it. The unexpected rage, the jitters, the indecision—all of it.

Hopefully, for you, moving day will go a lot smoother than it did for my client who had to move out of his family home. Here are a few heads up items to help your mental state during the actual move.

Prepare yourself mentally by knowing that the lifting of an old bed may cause old items laden in dust to trigger memories and emotions that have been buried for decades. Embrace it. The transition is happening as it is supposed to.

Invariably, when a couple moves into a new home, one partner leaves to pick up something at a nearby store, leaving the other with the movers. Now, the movers are asking the partner who stayed at the home a slew of questions: Where to put the rug? Should it be placed lengthwise or widthwise? Sometimes, the client turns to me—I've placed a lot of rugs in rooms—to ask what I think. But I know in advance that if the two of us agree on where it should go, the partner who went out will most likely return and decisively say, "Nope, the rug should go the other way."

It's all in a day of moving, when emotions run free.

I understand when nerves run high one client may want to disappear while another may want to "helicopter" the situation.

We have clients who don't want to be around at all during the move, and that's fine for restoration jobs, where there's water damage and you have to take everything out, then put it back in place after the work is done. We can easily photo-inventory it and create a 3D walkthrough so we know exactly how everything should be placed.

However, when you're moving from one house to another, a designer, organizer, or someone else needs to be there to act as a coordinator. Relocators requires its clients to sign a moving location release every time we leave a location. Whether your mover does or not is irrelevant. As the homeowner or renter, you should be the person to make sure everything you want is put on the truck. You should also check every area of the home you're leaving to ensure nothing is left behind and that what is left behind is supposed to be.

The last thing you want is a he-said/she-said situation where a mover wants to charge you to drive back for a lamp you told them to take in the first place. But there's a fine line. The clients need to be involved with the coordination but shouldn't be telling the movers how to load the truck or how to do their jobs. When a client becomes too involved and meddles, they can interfere with the flow of a move. It's better to trust the professionals, the expert movers who relocate people every day for a living. For example, movers know what to place in certain parts of the truck that are safer and will protect the items during transport.

Without the color-coding system, the client or point of contact has to point out where everything goes, and that's almost a foreman's job, which can turn out to be an entire job for the client. (See the Real-World Hacks section for more on the color-coding system.) The system saves time, and therefore money, for the client and the movers. In addition to the color-coding system, if you provide the movers with a diagrammed layout showing where all of the furniture goes in each room of the house, this also saves the movers having to ask the client where they want each piece of furniture to go.

THE REAL-WORLD HACKS

1. **Photographic evidence.** As they arrive, tell your movers which items are of high-value or sentimental importance. Take pictures of these items so there is a documented history of what they look like before the move. This catalog will be important if the items are damaged.

2. **Track your treasures.** Check again that you have all of your most personal and valued belongings either out of the house or clearly

marked and separated from the contents the movers will load into the truck.

3. **The essentials.** Determine which essential items to set aside. If there are three people in the house, you'll need three sets of dinnerware or paper plates and utensils, and perhaps a microwave and some leftover food. Be sure to include any medications you take regularly.

4. **Leave no stone unturned.** Search the corners and any hidden spots, including crawl spaces, attics, and other storage spaces in your home and property, as well as under the deck and in the garage or shed. You might have things you didn't realize you stored but wouldn't want to leave behind.

5. **Best-laid plans.** Confirm with your movers the day before that they will arrive as planned. The best movers will call to confirm with you. At this time, tell them if any last-minute changes have happened. Understand that additional legs to the trip can quickly drive up moving expenses.

    Whether you're dropping off a piano from your old home to a neighbor or picking up a dining table along the way to your new location, keep in mind that while these stops may be important to you, they will increase the cost of your move. Telling the movers during the move offsets the in-motion plan, so your best bet is to mention any changes as soon as you become aware of them.

6. **Entertainment value.** If you have kids, be sure to pack a bag with items, including any electronic devices and toys, that will keep them occupied on moving day.

7. **Pet essentials.** If you have pets, be sure to keep on hand all the essential items you need to care for them.

8. **Last goodbyes.** Say goodbye to the neighbors who mean something to you in advance. The last thing you want is for them to stop by on moving day wanting to have a long conversation.

9. **Color-code it.** Plan and allocate where each item will go in your new home. Some of my clients have color-coded their items, so that at the first location the items in the son's room are marked with a piece of blue tape, and there is a piece of blue paper or tape on the door of the son's room at the second location.

   You can purchase packs of colored tape to use for different rooms of the house. Make a list of the rooms and their corresponding colors, and when you arrive at the new location, tape a piece of colored paper or tape to the door of each room or on the wall beside the entrance. Tape each box accordingly, and tell your movers about the color code. It makes the job much easier and saves time when unloading. And remember, in moving, time is money.

10. **Fair-weather moves.** Keep an eye on the weather, making sure things are wrapped properly, and remember, rain and snow will make your move take that much longer.

11. **Local moves.** Make sure your movers are going with, not against, traffic when possible so you're not paying them to idle in rush-hour congestion. Moving time is calculated from the arrival at the first location until completion at the last location. Truck and travel time is from base to location and is usually a set standard hour. This means that the time from the first location to the second location is variable move time, and traffic can cause costs to run up.

12. **Long-distance moves.** Consider what day the unload will be. Usually, there is a broad time frame that can be from three to 10 or more days. Do you have a set date when you have to move in? This can increase the cost of the move, requiring you to pay extra

for the movers to work around your availability rather than based on their scheduling needs and operations.

13. **Point of contact.** For long-distance moves, let your mover know the point of contact and the best number to reach them, and ensure someone will be at the new home when the truck arrives.

14. **A soft landing.** Consider buying felt (those pre packaged felt circles that are sold everywhere) for the movers to apply to the bottom of your furniture while it's upside down so that when they position items in the new home, those items won't scuff wooden floors. This saves a lot of work you would have to do after the move.

15. **A better foundation.** Movers should put down Masonite or cardboard to protect floors.

16. **Set your priorities.** Determine which room should be set up first. Maybe you need to assemble your child's crib, or maybe the primary bedroom or kitchen is the first priority, or you need a recliner for an elderly parent or relative. Keep that in mind as the truck is loaded; the last items in the truck are the first to be unloaded.

17. **Can it.** Will the former homeowners leave their garbage pails, or do you need to buy new ones, and if so, do you have heavy duty contractor bags (3 mil) ready? As things are unwrapped, garbage piles up. Often a tip of appreciation and polite question will get you movers that will take away scrap wrappings.

18. **A change will do you good.** Change the locks, garage codes, and codes or locks for any pertinent entrance and exit routes immediately after moving in or just prior.

19. **Escape plans.** Study escape routes in case of fire. Add stickers to kids' windows for firemen; these fire rescue markers are available online and help firemen locate the rooms of children in a rescue situation. Check your basement egress and ensure every area of the new home has a double escape route.

20. **Don't void warranties.** Before you move, check warranties to find out if a licensed professional is required to move the item. The warranty may be voided otherwise.

THE CONCLUSION

Moving day is the day all your hard work will pay off. Keep a book or legal pad handy with all the items pertinent to help you get through this process. Remember that everything will not nor can be done in one day. Cross off your most important items. When you rest your head that night on your bed in your new home, be thankful the hard part is over and you have a homebase again. It will be some time before you really feel settled and your transition is completely through. Make sure you do not feel the stress of all that needs to be done and are reassured that you have all the time with little pressure to now settle in and replant your roots. Remember, although your moving stresses are real and significant, in reality they are high-class problems. Hundreds of millions of people around the globe do not have a roof over their head. Be thankful and take a deep breath. You have made it to the other side of the tunnel by reaching the "put everything back together" side of the transition.

To do or not to do, that is the question up next.

BONUS TIP: Plan before the move where you want things to go in your new home. I have seen hours wasted because clients ask movers to relocate large furniture four, five, even six times to figure out how a room should be decorated. Fun fact: if you're not hiring a decorator, use your head mover's advice. Movers are the world's best decorators because they arrange living spaces day in and day out. Pre-plan your furniture layout ahead of time and color-code pieces of furniture to designate which room they should go in. Take a sketch of the layout for each room to reference for the movers when they arrive in the new location.

BONUS TIP: Give your mover as many phone numbers as possible to reach the point person. This way, you save time, and remember—with moving, time is money.

MOVING DAY

THE EXPERTS

—Randy Goldbaum, Entrepenuer & Expert on Egress

"Code-compliant egress windows systems or walkouts are not only smart, they are a federal code. All basements with inhabitable spaces require two forms of egress. In addition to safety, an Egress emergency escape system provides a healthy living space and increased home value."

—Zendon Hamilton, NBA Former Player & Basketball Coach

"I will say this!
When you're an athlete, moving comes quite quickly and most of the time, it's unexpected, so it's always difficult, especially when it's unexpected, because the first things you think of are what I call The 4 Ps, which are:

- *Planning*
- *Packing*
- *People*
- *Planes*

Because you're going to encounter those specific things in the next two or three hours before you reach your next destination."

Final Day of Moving...

THE DO'S AND DON'TS OF WORKING WITH MOVERS

"The most expensive freebie always comes after saying: 'while you're here, could you just?'"

—Robert Esposito

MOVERS MOVE

One job we did was for a woman whose house was flooded and insurance was re-doing everything. We were tasked with wrapping and packing all her stuff and moving it into her garages. We had to move her fridge but it had a connected water line. We refused and came back the next day to move it into the garage only after she hired a plumber to disconnect the line. As movers, we do not do plumbing.

Months later we returned and placed the fridge four feet from where it was supposed to be pushed back into the pocket of her cabinets. We set the house back up and took pictures of everything including where we left the fridge. The client demanded we put the fridge completely back and we reminded her that we could not do the water line. We assured her that we would be back as soon as she had it professionally hooked up, to place it in the pocket it belonged. We did not hear from her for a week or so even after we called wondering why we did not have to put the fridge back.

Unbeknownst to us she had her house caretaker, who's not licensed, hook the fridge line back up and push the fridge back into the pocket. In doing so he kinked the line. The result? She submitted a second claim of approximately $50,000 to her homeowners insurance.

Even though we weren't responsible, she tried to say we had responsibility in the beginning for not completing a job we were not licensed to do. This just goes to show that movers shouldn't be taking apart dryers that have gas lines or anything like plumbing, electrical, hanging pictures or chandeliers, or HVAC. We can disassemble and reassemble furniture, and that's it. Given that we understand our limitations and clearly documented what we can and cannot do we had zero liability. Regardless of what she knew; the second move was contentious and on edge to say the least.

Sometimes when you're right, you're still wrong. I felt bad and I understood how ridiculous it may seem to not reattach a line. However, I have seen things happen a hundred times and when you do something you own it, especially when it is something you're not licensed to do.

The Bonus Story (Sorta!)

Handle with care

Mike was a new estimator. I had known him for years and was very happy when he joined the team. Mike is straight but it is questionable if you ask anyone who knows him. He is a grown man who jokes like a young teen. You know the type—if they grab a hotdog some dumb smirk and giggle will be on their face. I've had gay friends tell me their spidey senses engage when he is around. On his second week with the company, Mike walked in my office looking like he saw a ghost. I said, "What's up, are you okay?" He said, "Rob, I am a company man to the fullest but there is a point where I have to draw a line."

I asked what he was talking about. This is exactly what Mike responded with in his own words.

"So I knocked on the door and there was a nice gentleman in his pajamas. He was wearing a wife-beater tee and shorts. (In New York a wife beater tee is slang for white tank top undershirts) I told him I was here for the move estimate and he

shook my hand and greeted me. I regret the handshake but I did not know any better at the moment.

As we walked around from room to room I could swear I heard a low level thumping. It was almost like a humming sound but with a thump like bat, bat, bat, repeatedly. The vibe was weird and I figured I was just nervous because I am not used to being in peoples houses doing estimates. When we got to the kitchen he had a small TV on the kitchen table which was the source of the thumping I heard. I didn't think anything of it and then when I went to snap a picture I froze upon seeing gay porn on the TV. He caught my gaze and immediately said, 'it calms me, the spanking helps ease my anxiety.'

I try to be professional always, Rob, but I definitely was taken aback and he caught my quick stutter. I replied, 'different strokes for different folks,' which was a line I immediately regretted responding with. Which I made even worse by saying, 'I mean like whatever you're into, I respect it, I do not judge.'

I got right back to doing the estimate but the client clearly shifted his intentions. The last two rooms were awkward, but I stayed on task. As I said I would be sending his estimate he really did not pay attention to me. He was too focused on reopening the conversation about his relaxation techniques. He asked if I would like to stay. I said no thank you. He asked if I had any experience with being spanked, which I do not! He said he wouldn't mind showing me if I would like that. I said no thank you and stepped out the door very cordially. I did not shake his hand again but I did everything else right."

My only fathomable response was simple. "Thanks Mike, way to take one for the team!"

THE DO'S AND DON'TS OF WORKING WITH MOVERS

THE ADVICE

The movers you hire should be licensed as movers. If you happen to work with a mover who's also licensed in something like HVAC, electrical, plumbing, and so on, that's great and generally are a rare find and nonexistent. But to ensure the work that's done is covered—namely, that the company who repairs your leaky sink would cover the work that they do, should anything go wrong, so you don't have to pay to fix the same problem twice—hire a professional who is licensed in the work they're doing.

Don't ask your movers to uninstall the gas lines on the dryer just because they are able to. The phrase, "while you're here, could you just …" can cause you a lot more headaches than time or money saved. Make sure experts are doing what they specialize in when working in your home.

THE REAL-WORLD HACKS (DO'S & DON'TS STYLE)

1. **Don't** ask movers to hang TV's.

   Do have movers disassemble and reassemble furniture. Or, you can do this yourself, if you are able to, in order to save money.

2. **Don't** ask movers to hang art, mirrors, or pictures.

   Do have movers unwrap art and mirrors and place them carefully where you would like them hung.

3. **Don't** do half the move (content-wise) and pack all the easy items, expecting to save half the money. For movers, those items may account for very little of the moving time. (See Chapter 1: The Art of Selecting a Mover, for more on this.)

   Do ask the movers what you can do before the move to save the most time and money. Usually this includes disassembling and packing very fragile items.

4. **Don't** disappear without making sure someone is there to represent you at your home while the movers are there.

   Do make sure someone with knowledge of how you want things is available at all times throughout the move.

5. **Don't** let your movers leave a location without thoroughly checking it to make sure nothing is left behind.

   Do insist on walking through every room with the foreman at every location before the truck leaves the premises.

6. **Don't** ask movers to connect or disconnect anything electrical, like sconces, chandeliers, etc.

   Do hire a professional electrician before the move to disconnect anything electrical.

THE DO'S AND DON'TS OF WORKING WITH MOVERS

7. **Don't** ask movers to connect or disconnect water lines on refrigerators or anything else.

   Do coordinate a professional plumber ahead of time.

8. **Don't** ask movers to connect or disconnect barbecues or dryers with gas lines.

   Do hire a professional prior to the move, especially to connect and disconnect any gas lines.

9. **Don't** transport plants in the back of a moving truck.

   Do place plant pots in durable tubs and take them in a pick-up truck or personal car on local moves.

10. **Don't** move plants over state lines. There are strict plant regulations in many states prohibiting the import of certain species.

    Do give away regional plants locally and purchase new ones from the region you're moving to.

11. **Don't** move temperature-controlled items, like perishable food, in a moving truck.

    Do bring as few perishable items as possible during the move. You can give any remaining food to friends, family, or neighbors and pack anything you want to take with you in coolers, which are best transported in a personal vehicle.

12. **Don't** have movers pack or move money, jewelry, coins, firearms, ammunition, or precious metals.

    Do keep all valuable items under lock and key and securely lock them in your vehicle or leave them with a family member.

13. **Don't** pack flammable items on a moving truck.

    Do responsibly dispose of flammable items and anything you can't take on a moving truck.

14. **Don't** hire an uninsured mover. You can ask to see their certificate of insurance if you would like proof.

    Do get at least three estimates from licensed, insured movers.

15. **Don't** insist on making something fit against the advice of the mover unless you don't care about the potential resulting issues, like a stained wall or damaged drywall.

    Do consider changing your intended locations for furniture and other items by analyzing the path of least resistance. If you insist on items going to certain places, consider the costs of repair before making the decision.

16. **Don't** leave fragile items and boxes containing breakables scattered throughout the home; instead, stage them in a certain area. If possible, place all mirrors, glass shelving, and other furnishings with breakable pieces in the same area of the home before the movers arrive.

    Do place all boxes containing fragile items together in a specific area and let the movers know where they are before they load the truck.

17. **Don't** allow anyone, licensed or unlicensed, to work in your home if the homeowner's insurance is not active.

    Do keep homeowner's insurance current at all times while you own your home.

18. **Don't** store a fridge or freezer that is not plugged in without leaving the doors wide open, or better yet, removing the doors.

    Do empty all ice and water and dry all condensation from fridges and freezers, then remove doors while the fridge is not plugged in.

19. **Don't** have any expectations of pressboard furniture making it to the second location intact or being reimbursed for it. It is not reimbursable or made for moving.

THE DO'S AND DON'TS OF WORKING WITH MOVERS

Do stretch-wrap joints, then wrap them again for the best possible results of moving pressboard furnishings. However, it's realistic to have no expectations of such furniture arriving intact.

20. **Don't** interfere with the movers while they're working, especially when they're carrying large or heavy items.

    Do guide the foreman without interfering with his expertise.

21. **Don't** leave bulbs in lamps or lampshades on lamps.

    Do remove and pack light bulbs and lampshades. It's also a good idea to purchase and pack plenty of light bulbs for your new home and make sure to have extra on hand.

22. **Don't** leave fuel in gasoline-powered equipment. Be sure to drain it prior to the move.

    Do double- and triple-check all equipment for fuel before moving.

23. **Don't** let your movers move any electronics without having them sign off to confirm that they're aware the item was working properly. MCU means mechanical condition unknown and if they never saw the electronics on and working, and you signed off on an MCU-listed item, you may unknowingly void coverage.

    Do turn on all electronics and take pictures or videos showing them in their working condition.

24. **Don't** neglect to tip your movers; between 10% of the total move, divided amongst the men. Tips are split amongst all workers, with the foreman receiving the lion's share.

    Do use discretion and tip based on performance and service received.

25. **Don't** forget to measure doorways and other entries into the house. There's nothing worse than finding out there's no way to bring your refrigerator or favorite couch into your new home.

    Do review openings and egresses prior to bringing items into a house and planning the placement of items in a room.

26. **Don't** forget to measure the rooms in the new location to aid in planning the layout.

    Do take into consideration windows and feng shui principles when planning the layout of rooms.

27. **Don't** make boxes too heavy when you pack. Not only are they harder to lift, but the box may not hold up during the move. Pack heavier items, like books, in multiple smaller boxes.

    Do label all heavy boxes to avoid startling, surprising, or hurting laborers.

28. **Don't** forget to mark fragile all boxes containing breakable and delicate items.

    Do double-check that all boxes containing fragile items are labeled.

29. **Don't** leave boxes scattered in different areas of the house. To make the moving process go faster, consolidate all boxes into one room or central area that is easy for movers to access.

    Do make sure walkways are clear of boxes and show movers where items are placed in the home before they start loading the truck.

30. **Don't** forget to check that nothing was left on the moving truck after it's unloaded.

    Do check the truck at each location after unloading to ensure nothing is left. Pick up folded blankets to check for mistakenly hidden items.

31. **Don't** assume your certificate of insurance is accepted after you've sent it. Confirm that it's been approved and everything (such as elevator reservations) can proceed as planned and on schedule.

    Do get written email approval from the building management and keep it on hand during the move as proof.

32. **Don't** leave your significant other to tell the movers where things go, unless you've provided them with a layout beforehand. As

THE DO'S AND DON'TS OF WORKING WITH MOVERS

recommended elsewhere in this book, it's even better to provide an agreed-upon layout to the movers as soon as they arrive.

Do give a copy of the layout to your significant other in case you have to leave the premises.

33. **Don't** forget to change the locks and any access codes for your new home to ensure your safety.

    Do coordinate a locksmith to change any locks on day one of living in your new home.

34. **Don't** forget to bring with you any artifacts or items of religious significance from your old home, especially if those items are outside. For example, Italians bury a statue of St. Joseph to help sell houses. Don't forget to pack St. Joseph!

    Do ask any family members if they have hidden anything over the years that might be easily overlooked.

35. **Don't** wait until after you've moved in to paint or replace flooring. Whenever possible, take care of these things beforehand to ease the transition.

    Do keep items out of the room that need immediate touch-ups or repairs.

36. **Don't** place barbecue grills too close to the home, as they can ignite a little more than your burgers.

    Do keep barbeque grills on a cement pad away from any other items that could catch fire.

37. **Don't** assume that when you have a gap closing, your items need to go into storage or transit storage, which may be provided by your mover. If your new home is closing days after the home you're selling, it will cost thousands to unload and reload items into storage. Moving companies may charge up to $500 a night to store items on the truck. If you're on good terms with the homebuyer or if you ask your attorney, you may be able to get the homeowner you're

buying the house from to allow the movers to drop all items in the garage or basement, and leave any outdoor items in the yard. This is also beneficial if you need to do quick renovations but have to be out of the first house. Hiring people to place items in a garage is always cheaper than unloading and reloading items into storage or using transit storage.

Do explain the whole scenario to the expert (your moving company) and ask about the best possible solutions for the moving gap.

38. **Don't** compare prices; compare costs. An estimate is only that—an estimate—and even an expert can be wrong. Moving quotes usually include ranges or probable cost sections that are higher than estimates. People often assume estimates reflect the final cost and are surprised when it turns out to be different. A lower quoted service amount could be a trap to get a job and then hold the client hostage. Don't compare on-site estimates to phone estimates, as on-site estimates tend to be more accurate in reflecting a price that's closer to the actual, final cost.

Do read this entire book before moving and refer to the Good vs. Cheap vs. Fast section in Chapter 1: The Art of Selecting a Mover.

THE DO'S AND DON'TS OF WORKING WITH MOVERS

THE CONCLUSION

As you have seen throughout this book moving is much more personal than other trades. This often causes movers to be asked things outside the scope of moving. This often happens because they are in the house working closely and a more trusting bond develops. This is by all means a good thing. However, it is important to note that just because someone can do something it does not necessarily mean that they should. Paying a little more to hire a licensed handyman to hang precious art, or an electrician to hang sconces; will always be the safer option.

> **BONUS TIP:** Many movers don't insure things they don't pack themselves, such as fragile items. Don't forget to ask the moving company about what they will and will not insure before you pack. It's also good to know what their insurance covers. Ideally, a moving company should insure the belongings they move (though they may not insure items they didn't pack, so check with them on this). They should also carry general liability insurance.

QUICK PRELUDE TO TRANSITIONAL SERVICES

> "Whoever you are, or whatever it is that you do, when you really want something, it's because that desire originated in the soul of the universe. It's your mission on earth."
>
> —Paulo Coelho, The Alchemist

THE ADVICE

While I understand the world is far from perfect; I would like to take a moment to explain the perfect scenario. Of course downsizing, and an estate, almost always require more than two services. Even the smallest moves could require multiple services. I designed Relocators to be an end to end solution by combining all of the transitional services. The industry as a whole is fragmented and multiple companies will be needed to handle the entire transition in most cases. If ever you find yourself needing all or some of these services due to the need to transition out of a house, this is how you should best proceed in a "perfect world."

THE DO'S AND DON'TS OF WORKING WITH MOVERS

THE REAL-WORLD HACKS (10 STEP RELO ROAD MAP STYLE)

1. Set a date with all family or friends that may have a stake in an item in the home. Tell them this is the deadline for them to declare what they want.

2. Label all items people are taking and items that have to stay in the home.

3. Hire an estate sale company.

4. Get a clean-out estimate as if the clean-out were to be done the following day.

5. Schedule and execute the movers to move all the wanted items into storage or directly to their second locations.

6. Execute and complete the sale or auction.

7. Allow any neighbors, family, or friends, to come take for free any items that did not sell. At this step, you can also donate items. This is when you do as much or as little as you prefer to mitigate the final clean-out costs.

8. Ask for an updated clean-out estimate.

9. Execute clean-out so home is "walk through ready."

10. At your convenience, call for items to be shipped out-of-state or to second locations, if you had them moved into storage.

SELLING ITEMS- ESTATE SALES & ONLINE AUCTIONS

"Someone is sitting in the shade today because someone planted a tree a long time ago."

-Warren Buffet

THIEVES IN CLIENTS CLOTHING

Once, a customer of ours, like so many, had inherited her childhood home after her parents had passed away. She had lived next door to them in her adult life and was extremely emotional about the entire situation. She was an only child and had no reason to sustain both houses after her parents had passed on.

We decided on an online auction as opposed to an estate sale because it is less intrusive. With estate sales hundreds if not thousands of people show up for a one or two day blow out sale. Auctions are calmer and more controlled. With auctions we send in our staff to photograph everything. Everything is then purchased via credit card on a third party website over the course of two weeks. The pick up of items is a set four hour window where only our staff bring each lot out to the respective buyer.

We went through the entire house and photographed approximately 500 lots of merchandise. The customer was extremely appreciative the whole time, loved everything, and praised me on how compassionate I was toward her and her parents' belongings. That candor went on for about two weeks, almost all of the prepping period.

When the auction went live, I could see her emotions continuing to build, but she was still okay with selling the items. On the last day of the auction, as it was about to end, she called me and said she wanted to cancel the auction. She said we could keep the money she'd paid us

SELLING ITEMS-ESTATE SALES & ONLINE AUCTIONS

so far and that she didn't want to sell her parents' items. Out of 500 items on auction, over 400 already had bids placed, which meant that the bidders' credit cards had charges. There was no possible way for us to cancel the auction.

I spent three hours on the phone with her calming her down. It goes without saying but once an auction is live, and there are bids, there is absolutely no contractual or logistical way to end an auction. Regardless, she needed to sell the items anyway. Her closing was the following week. She cried, she yelled at me, she cursed me, she cried some more. She cursed some more and then finally, she let go and agreed to proceed.

The auction ended and there was a tremendous pick-up at her house that Saturday. It was about 100 degrees outside. We arrived at the house for the pick-up and found that she had scattered every single item throughout the house. I had lined up over 200 Lionel trains in a bedroom, which I discovered she'd put in five different boxes. She'd removed all the inventory stickers and had moved every small item into different rooms; she'd even removed items. We were trying to pull the invoices, preparing for the people to show up by 11 a.m. We were expecting approximately 300 people. By 10:30 a.m., the line outside was already about 100 people long. Imagine holding over 450 invoices with pre-purchased items all perfectly left for easy management. Then showing up to find the entire arrangement at the point of being boobie trapped. Absolute disaster!

The customer sat in the corner and wouldn't talk to anyone. Once she realized how many people were outside, she took a lawn chair, sat in the driveway, and yelled at each and every winning bidder, saying they were thieves and they were taking her parents' items. She was spitting at them, and yelling personal insults at them. She looked like a full-blown psychopath.

I asked her time and time again if she'd like to leave. I said I'd go get coffee with her and asked if she'd like to go for a walk, but nothing was working. She just continued to get more and more irate. Meanwhile, the line kept getting longer because we couldn't find anything in the house. All of a sudden, the skies opened up and it began to pour. She was soaking wet, still yelling at everyone, and about 200 people in line all the way down the block were now yelling at me. I walked to the backyard, stood in the corner, and contemplated just leaving because I didn't see an end to it. I was trapped, this was all on me and I could not figure a way to get out of this. It felt like my world was crumbling.

Finally, I took a few deep breaths, went back inside, and just put the blinders on, rallied my team and got things done. At the end of the day, she said with the snarkiest tongue, "I hope you're happy with yourself." I said goodbye and expected to never hear from her again. I prepped other management at work to prepare for defense with whatever negative reviews or backlash we were about to receive from her.

The next day, she texted me thanking me (never apologizing) and asked if there was a rain check on our coffee date. It was the worst experience I've ever had in a work environment. All of this is completely fueled by an emotional reaction to an event that by all other parameters is something most of us need to go through as a part of life.

THE ADVICE

Imagine all the emotions when it comes time to empty a childhood home especially after the loss of a parent. Memories, death, sibling rivalries, in-laws, unfinished childhood feuds, mourning, and all the mayhem that comes with family all rolled up into one event. An event that consists of the culmination of the home where everything began for you.

All of this emotion and chaos and the stress from the physical act of removing stuff from the home has yet to even begin.

Over the years I have come up with a model of three personalities that I believe always appears when a parent passes away. Whether there are one or ten adult children in a family is irrelevant. When a parent passes, a combination of three personalities always shows up: the caretaker, the executor, and the apathetic one. From an imbalance of shared responsibilities to the challenges among siblings—no matter if there is only one child—these three personality types are nearly always present.

Consider the caretaker, the one who rightfully feels entitled because they did all the "real work" while the parent was alive. Caretakers spend years making sure parents are hydrated, fed, and clean. They run to the doctor with them and help with the most intimate of tasks. In a sense, it comes full circle because the care of the child for the parent reflects the care the child received from the parent. But the caretaker never once charged the estate for all the hours they put in. How could they, after all their parents had sacrificed for them? That perspective always seems to change once the parent dies. Most of the time, the caretaker is stunned to find out that all of that work they would not dare bill for, now cannot be billed. Had they billed the care while the parent was alive they could have been compensated. Yet, the so-called real work counts for nothing when it comes to the will, (pun intended) both the parent's will and the documented legal will. I'm talking here about both the parent's wishes for the children they are leaving behind and the legal document the parent left to settle the estate. The parent may have done everything right with the legal document, but still, the sheer reality of a parent's death often causes chaos. As the caretaker often discovers, the real work does not count when it comes to the will.

Then there's the executor. They make all the big decisions, only to find they are resented, especially when another family member wants to bring their financial expertise into the equation.

And then there's the apathetic one, the person who doesn't seem to care about anything. Maybe this person tends to hide emotions and deals with things differently than the other siblings. They just want the estate buttoned up so they can get their share of the inheritance, hop on a plane, and get back home, relieved for the distance from their family. Their love may not be less; it's just different. It could be said that they "love from afar."

These personalities can trigger drama. There are fights between siblings. Some try to build alliances and team up against another brother or sister about who is really owed what and entitled to which possessions when divvying up the property. These scenarios create more stress and tension, even if the will of the loved one who passed was all about keeping the family united so they could move forward together. The event of their death in itself has the siblings on the brink of separation.

I've seen so many situations that represent the three personalities. In one case, there were three brothers. One brother moved the mother, whose health was starting to fail, into his house. The mother, helping with the money and decisions, purchased, with him, a car. He took care of her for several years.

One brother lived out of state, and the other lived nearby but was never really there for their mother, other than for significant holidays. The brother who helped her buy the car spent all the time with her—late nights getting up to help, taking her to doctor's visits, and so on. He spent all those years nursing her and then she went into hospice.

She died a few months later but in those few months, the son that was caring for her sold the new car that the mother owned, as he was the executor and the caretaker in this instance, to his daughter. His two brothers were never given the choice or the option to buy the car.

Ideally this situation could be avoided. Everyone else has to be involved in those questions. But because the brother who took care of their mother was the executor of the estate and it wasn't an estate yet, he was able to sell the car to his daughter. His daughter got a fair deal on the car and the other two siblings received their portion of the proceeds. However, the other brothers didn't have the option to buy it and one of the brothers wound up suing him. The other brother, upon hearing this, wiped out the mother's bank account because he happened to be a signer on the account. Neither the brothers nor their children, (the other grandchildren) were given the right of refusal. By playing favorites with his own daughter, the executor, in essence, alienated his whole family against him and his daughter.

When the parent is alive, the one with that caretaker, nurturing side would never charge their parent to clean them or take care of them because their parent took care of them as a child. But the moment the parent dies, they resent the fact that their siblings didn't help. They start saying, "I worked all those hours. I deserve more." They're entitled and rightfully so; they did do all the real work. But the real work doesn't count in the will, unless they submitted hours during the time they were performing caretaker duties. They can't go back now after the parent has passed and claim the money. Then a rift begins. And if another sibling comes in who's in accounting or finance and they find out in the will that they're the executor, that typically widens the rift. There's always one sibling who says, "Stop fighting, just sell it. I need the money." They miss their parent, but they don't show it like the other siblings do, for whom every piece of jewelry and every couch is a memory.

There are going to be setbacks that flare up as loved ones fight it out. Yet the need to pack up the home still looms.

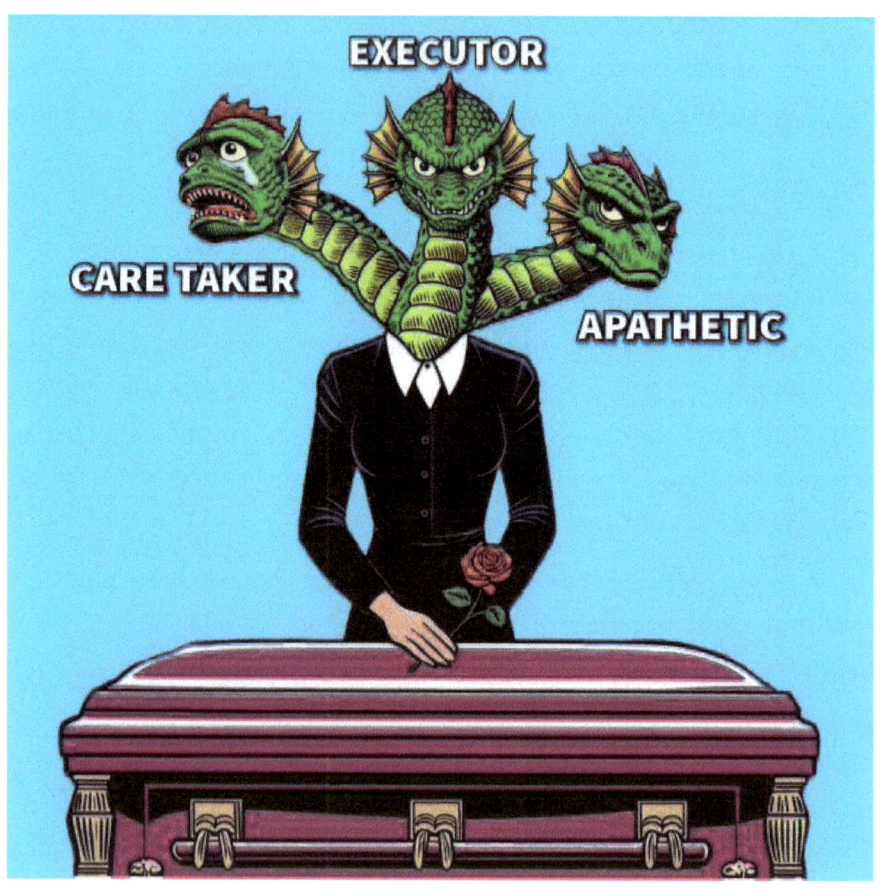

THE REAL-WORLD HACKS

1. **Last call.** If you're having an estate sale, before you call an estate sale company, if you're going to retain one, decide with siblings and anyone else who may have a stake in the estate on a hard date that works for everyone. This provides a last opportunity to have items spoken for.

2. **Time-saver.** If you think you might have an estate sale, only go through areas of the house where there might be something you want to keep. Don't waste time organizing items you're sure you don't want.

3. **Trash or treasure.** The estate-sale expert will determine if there is enough for an in-person estate sale or an online auction. Typically, the total value of the items you're offering for sale should be at least $5,000. It doesn't matter if you have tons of low-valued items, and only a few high-end pieces for sale. Usually, a mix of items at different price points works best. And while I've seen some online auctions bring in as much as $90,000, the average ones bring in between $4,000 and $12,000.

4. **Save it.** Don't throw anything out before the sale. People love nostalgic stuff, especially items that are in original boxes. And you might never know when something is valuable. I'm reminded of an auction Relocators handled. The items included some old, dusty lamps. In the last hour, they sold them for $36,000. They turned out to be from the Ming Dynasty, and two Chinese nationals got into a bidding war over them.

5. **Abiding by the agreement.** If you sign on with an estate sale company, people might start asking for first dibs. Do not give away or sell anything on your own. The company has agreed to market and sell your items, which are cataloged and assessed, and their

credibility is at stake. Once it's marketed, they've assumed responsibility to get the highest possible price for the items. Tell any friends or family who request items that it's all up to the estate sale company now—this will also absolve you of any uncomfortable situations and conversations.

6. **Observations.** Before deciding on an estate sale company, go to some of their sales and observe how they conduct them.

7. **Consider your options.** If there isn't enough inventory to conduct a sale, the company should give you some options. I constantly bring in appraisers or antique dealers for clients who have specific items that might be worth money but aren't enough to hold a sale. At the very least, I try to lead them in a good direction and offer our donation and cleanout service to get their home closing-ready.

8. **Spread the word.** If you don't have an estate sale, get the word out to as many people as you can about the items you no longer want. Post them on social media and tell your neighbors about the items. List them on your preferred website, but be careful of strangers and lower-end websites. Do not post unless you feel secure and take the proper precautions. This may include only meeting strangers when someone else accompanies you, only meeting during the day, and only posting pictures of specific items and not whole rooms. Pictures of an entire room could possibly intrigue the wrong person looking for something in the background.

9. **Protect your valuables.** Before the sale, separate the valuable items. Lock up any jewelry, whether you're holding an estate sale or an online auction. When Relocators handle an estate sale, we set up the home like a department store. We put all valuable items close to the register in protected cases.

10. **Timing is everything.** Don't give out the address of an estate sale until two days before the sale because people sometimes camp out

for days to be the first ones in the home. These sales can bring in hundreds of people.

11. **Extra, extra! Read all about it!** If you're hosting a sale yourself, advertise it in the newspaper; people who go to sales look for those ads. Stake a lot of bright signs with arrows on every major road directing people to your sale. Be sure to have someone in each room of your home to keep an eye on things and answer any questions from potential buyers. Have just one entrance and exit in and out of the home.

12. **Take it online.** Online auctions are a little different. They were very popular during COVID, but traditionally, they are for the person who's living in a complex, a gated community, or a building that can't have an in-person sale. Others prefer online auctions because they don't want hundreds of people traipsing through their homes telling people that their items aren't worth anything. When Relocators conducts online auctions, we take pictures and catalog everything in the home. We post the items on a third-party auction site, which runs the auction for up to 14 days. At the end, all the credit cards have been captured. The moment the auction is over, we come back with staff and provide a four-hour window, where buyers bring in their invoices and we match the items. Or, we can ship the items.

13. **Fix it first.** Repair any hazardous conditions, like loose floorboards or rickety staircases before the sale to protect everyone who will be in the house. If that isn't possible, let the estate sale company know about any such conditions before the sale so they can take precautionary measures.

14. **Protect what's yours.** Before the sale, remove personal items, sensitive documents, cash and financial instruments (such as checks and traveler's checks), and any valuables that are not being sold in the estate sale.

15. **Location, location, location.** Large and heavy items, such as furniture, exercise equipment, and pianos, tend to sell faster when they're placed on the ground floor.

16. **Let the signs lead the way.** Make sure you or the company hang a lot of signs throughout your home: Watch Your Step, Icy Stoop, Watch Your Head, Sharp Objects, More This Way, Do Not Enter, etc.

17. **A treasure hunter's paradise.** Do not clean garages and attics with years of accumulation. There is an entire subculture of treasure hunters that go to estate sales every weekend. They sometimes camp out and wait to be first in line. They are all about the treasure hunt; cleaning 50 years of accumulation becomes counterproductive because they get incredibly excited when they see a "dig."

18. **Reminder.** I mention this throughout the book, but when having an estate sale, it is even more crucial to make sure your homeowner's insurance is active. It may even be worth it to call your insurance broker and ask if you can put a rider on your policy for the week of the estate sale. A small expense could lead to tremendous savings, if, God forbid, something were to happen.

19. **Lotto ticket.** We all have heard the stories of a very high valued item being found and sold for an accidental amazing bargain at a garage sale. They come off as old wives tales, but I assure you they are true. Prior to having a sale a great idea for a small investment would be to have a trusted antique dealer, or auctioneer, do a quick walk through your home to ensure there is nothing of immense value. This can also be the sales company you hire if they have the extensive knowledge. We have the knowledge and I still bring one in often if we suspect someone might have something but are not sure. Just to make sure our clients are well taken care of.

THE CONCLUSION

I knew all of the information I'm sharing with you before I started Relocators. When my nana was diagnosed with cancer back in the early 2000s, it was left to my mother to empty her house. My mom spent weekend after weekend renting dumpsters and enlisting friends to help her liquidate all of the contents. She recognized that selling the stuff would help bring money in as well as limit waste and help repurpose important things for those in need, and once she did it for herself, she figured she could help others, too.

So, she posted an ad in the local paper that read, "Old stuff out, brings the money in. Let us show you where to begin." This was when she launched Sisters in Charge, an estate sale business. She'd bring in hundreds of people who spent thousands of dollars at the sale before her clients finally sold their homes and moved. But her clients had so much more to do after the estate sale as they got ready to move. They had to get their residences closing-ready—all the belongings removed and the home broom-clean—by the closing date. It's a big job. But at my mom's recommendation, her clients started hiring me to get it done. It was a lot of work, but for me, a kid in college at the time, the money was good.

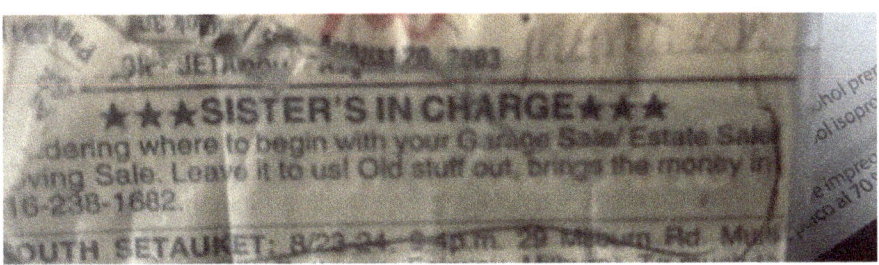

Many of the clients were going into assisted living facilities, and the facility directors began to refer business to me, which gave me the idea to start Relocators and offer an end-to-end solution for helping people to transition out of their homes. This helped me to grow my company. I began providing the services I knew they needed. These included clean-outs and junk removal, moving, secure storage, and later, restoration pack-outs, out-of-state moving, online auctions, and more.

During the time I helped with my mother's estate sale business, I received an in-the-trenches education about the process, which I'm sharing here to help you get closing-ready.

There are many times when people have canceled plane tickets after speaking with me. The realtor refers us for one of our services, then after talking with us, the clients feel comfortable after we explain our process and decide they do not need to take the trip or that they do not have to make the trip right away. In some instances, a neighbor or friend may also refer us and we would actually help them pick the realtor.

Before doing anything, give everyone with rights to the items a deadline to mark, move out, or claim what they're keeping.

Do not waste a second throwing anything out or going through areas of the home cleaning out cabinets and closets. People often spend weeks doing this, but there are only two reasons to go through a house or move things around:

1. You want to be sure there is nothing you want in that closet.
2. You want to be sure there is no hidden cash or high-value items in that closet.

If those two don't apply, you're wasting your time if your plan is to hire a professional. If you're doing it to save money and lower costs of services, that's okay. But it's better not to go through anything until you consult with a professional. Sales are based on quantity and quality and throwing things away can ultimately disqualify an estate sale company from taking on your sale.

Another important word of advice is not to tell anyone besides family (and close friends that are like family) about the upcoming sale. Don't tell neighbors or the new homeowners about it.

If you do decide to tell the new homeowners, that should be done before hiring an estate sale company. For houses with decent furniture, your path of least resistance could be to sell it all to the new homeowners, especially if they're first-time homebuyers who need it. Hiring an estate sale company could cost up to 40 to 50% of the items sold, so it is a great chance to give a nice break to a young family that could use it.

For neighbors, rarely does any good come out of telling them about the sale. Although I recommend fostering great relationships with neighbors, this is the one area where it's better to keep them in the dark, unless it's neighbors that have become like family. But again, that should be done prior to the deadline you've set for people to claim anything they want from the estate. The reason for this is that when you tell your mom's so-called best friend of 50 years, she suddenly absolutely can't live without mom's Lladró collection. Now what? You have to beg the estate sale company to allow you to break the contract for the so-called "friend" mom wasn't very fond of for the last 50 years.

Your best bet is to call any neighbors you decide to tell about the sale a few days before it's held. My advice is to call them from your faraway home and say you just want to give them a quick heads-up about the sale. If they respond negatively, you're not there, and they can be the first one on line to buy anything they want. You can always say you wish they had told you they wanted those items sooner.

BONUS TIP: Many estate sale companies ask the client to remain off-property during the sale. Even though it's their home and their or their family's belongings that are being sold, the client's presence can have an adverse effect on buyers and on those conducting the sale. An estate sale can evoke strong emotions from the client, especially if it's being held after a loved one has passed. Hire a company you trust to do the job effectively to make you feel more at ease when you're not there during the process.

THE EXPERT

Jeanine Gagliano - Right at Home South Shore Long Island

Right at Home provides in-home care to the elderly wherever they call home. We are often called by families when a loved one is moving into an assisted living community to provide advocacy and companionship. The stress and emotional toll of moving doesn't always end when the last box is unpacked. Seniors can feel lonely and intimidated trying to navigate, figuratively and physically, their new environment. I've heard a few of my clients liken it to their first day at a new school. Hiring a companion from an agency like Right at Home ensures that the senior participates in available activities, attends meals, and becomes acquainted with their surroundings. This eases the transition for not only the senior, but their family because there is someone there to provide feedback on how the client is feeling and assimilating. It may be counterintuitive, but in these types of cases the best news we can hear is that since the client is happy and thriving, our services are no longer needed!

Sandi Polinsky - Owner Goldilocks Realty

Not all elderly parents choose to sell their forever home. Some elderly parents choose to downsize. Whether for health, maintenance and upkeep, safety, or other reasons. I advise children of parents who opt to downsize to walk out the parent on the last day, holding their hand, when they close up the house.

The gift here is that your children can remember their forever home, walking their parents out in a healthy way onto their next chapter. In contrast, adult children that have to clear out belongings after a parent has passed will find it's very difficult due to the memories that were made in childhood.

STORAGE 7

"Stuff has become the enemy. There always seems to be more of it than I have storage in my house!"

—Rick Riordan

Locked Inside the Fortress

I've been locked in storage units so often, it's almost become a regular occurrence. Getting stuck on an elevator is commonplace. There have been times when the elevator didn't work, so we couldn't finish the job without using the stairs. God forbid you have something in the elevator when the power goes off—that's happened to us a lot. We have worked long twelve hour days of non stop lifting, finally ending at 10 p.m. in a storage facility, only to discover on leaving the storage facility that the electronic gate was closed for the night. This meant our truck was stuck inside the gates and we had to hop the fence and get a ride home with the client. We had to go back the next morning for the truck as soon as the storage facility opened. With most storage facilities, the gate closing time is more of a guideline you don't have to follow, but certain ones are automated. That rule is automatically set, but you don't know which ones have gates that close automatically and which don't.

The word *move* in itself is a verb which, when you think about it, implies not stopping or stepping aside. So besides the storage facilities, as movers, we are not used to being stuck in one place. However, one time we worked on a high-end restoration job where a building was burned because a billionaire set it ablaze. The fire was caught quickly so the damage wasn't terrible and a lot of the contents were salvageable. All of the penthouses just had smoke damage. Months later, we re-visited the site to return the items from storage and back into one of the penthouses. We were about halfway through the move when all of a sudden, the Feds arrived. Somebody had threatened to jump. They locked the building down for approximately eight hours. During that time, we had two guys stuck outside, the move half-done, and two guys stuck inside. One of the guys stuck inside was five years out of a very long prison sentence. He came from a very good reference and was eager to get his life together. We were happy to give him a second chance as he interviewed very well. We often find that on low-end labor jobs, people who are genuinely looking for a second chance in life usually are the most concrete, honest, dependable people you can count on in those jobs.

But in this scenario the guy was terrified. He was trapped unable to move for an indefinite amount of time in a building swarming with Feds and emergency services. The FBI locked down the building and allowed for no movement in or out. We had our share of fun making jokes about the employee stuck with all the law enforcement.

What a waste of a day. Nothing we could do. We were stuck the entire time. What do you do? Moving's billed at hourly rates.

THE ADVICE

To Store or Not to Store?

If you're moving, downsizing, handling an estate move, or just running out of space in general, you may be inclined to take out a storage unit. Storage and moving go together like peas and carrots; excuse my Forrest Gump reference. Three popular types of storage are self-storage, movers storage, and portable-on-location storage. Self-storage uses the big box facilities you see all across America. They offer affordable space in climate and non-climate controlled facilities. They are typically assembled using aluminum dividers with roll up doors as partitions. Self-storage facilities are completely DIY, most access is automated and the facilities themselves have very little staff.

Movers storage is warehousing at a facility run by a moving company. They are usually laid out using industrial racking or wooden crates that hold all the items in a self-contained, sealed manner. Movers storage is usually not accessible at all times; access is by appointment only. Movers storage is a great option because unlike the do-it-yourself application of self-storage, with movers storage a simple phone call can have your items stored or returned from storage. No need for client involvement when moving time comes.

Unlike the first two options, portable storage is usually not climate-controlled when stored on location. Portable storage is when companies put containers on your property and allow you to pay a low monthly fee to keep it on site, usually while work is being done. Portable storage is also somewhat of a DIY option. Portable can also be used to move items long distances. In this case, while the items are at the facility they usually would be in a climate-controlled environment.

Each storage option has a different application and, most of the time depending on a client's needs, one option could be best for that client or that specific situation. If you are hiring a company to move you into storage storage movers is almost always the best option. Packaging the job together makes it easier and less costly. However, if you are putting it in storage and you need to access the items regularly then, in this case, self-storage would be your best option. If you have a small amount of stuff and traveling a small distance, then in some instances hiring a company to load a portable storage and then hiring a different company to unload the portable storage at the destination may be a better option. Each application depends on the circumstances.

What is most important is what you should consider when renting a storage space.

THE REAL-WORLD HACKS

1. **My why.** Make sure to ask why you are storing items. Some reasons are obvious, like a gap in closing. Other reasons such as an emotional bond to a deceased relative's items, or to sell items, may not be the best economical decisions. Make sure you're clear on your purpose. In most instances, people should reconsider storing items because of an emotional bond, which will cost them financially.

   In addition, don't store to sell, unless the items are of such high value that the sale outweighs the storage costs. I do understand storing because of an emotional bond, and everyone has the right to spend money the way they choose. I would just recommend having a completion plan. I have seen many instances where an emotional bond keeps items in storage for over a decade, only for those items to be thrown away after all those years.

2. **Preservation is key.** Will you be storing items that are temperature-sensitive, like musical instruments, wooden furniture and electronics? If so, climate-controlled storage is your best bet.

3. **Keep it safe.** If valuable items are going into storage, choosing a facility with good security will be important.

4. **Timber..** Be cautious of how you stack items in storage. The last thing you want is a vibration to cause all your items to fall over and you not find out for months or years.

5. **Cover your bases.** Does the facility offer insurance to protect your items? If not, do you have a renter's or homeowner's insurance policy

that will cover them? Be very conscientious about understanding how the insurance policy works.

6. **Money, money, money.** Before you sign on with the storage facility, find out if you will have a locked-in rate or if they will be raising the rates periodically. If so, find out at what percent and time frame.

7. **All for a fee.** Many facilities offer the first month free or at a discounted rate. Ask about any special deals they're offering. Also find out if there are any hidden fees and make sure to ask what the actual monthly cost will be, as it reflects on your statement.

8. **Location, location, location.** If you live in an urban area, you may be able to take advantage of significant savings by choosing a facility outside the city.

9. **Hours of operation.** Find out what the hours are, both for the office and the facility access. Some facilities may post certain hours to make it seem like their office is open later than it really is.

10. **Ease of access.** Ask to see the storage unit you'll be getting before you sign any paperwork. If your unit is on the third floor, down a series of hallways, and accessible by a small elevator, this can affect the time and therefore the cost of the move.

11. **Three days grace?** It can be useful to know when the payment is considered late. Unlike rent payment, many storage facilities consider the payment late after the first day it's due and do not offer a grace period.

12. **Lost in space.** Consider the cubic feet of the storage unit and whether or not your items will fit. Cutting it too close can result in you having to rent another unit or make tough decisions on what to keep, discard, donate, or sell. Don't forget to take the unit's ceiling height into account and make sure your items will fit. It can be helpful to make a list of all storage items and to take measurements of them, once everything is packed, before choosing the unit size.

You can calculate cubic feet by multiplying length times width times height (LxWxH).

13. **Appearances aren't everything, but…** Is pest control provided and how often? Is the facility clean and well-maintained? Some storage facilities can fall to seedy activities, similar to low-end motel rooms. These circumstances just lead to more risk of others violating rules that can affect your items, even though they are separated.

14. **Educate yourself.** Are there any items that the facility does not allow you to store? Ensuring you're in compliance before you sign on the dotted line can save you headaches later. Familiarizing yourself with their rules and regulations beforehand is a good idea. Anything organic like perishable foods or plants should never be stored.

15. **Closing time.** I have been locked inside facility gates many times. They close at a posted time but it's easy to lose track of time or think, "No problem; no one is here anyway and the office is closed," only to find out the hard way that the electronic gates or elevators shut off at a specific time, creating a fortress.

16. **Keeping track.** If you are putting things in storage, make sure all of the contents are inventoried. Keep a copy of the inventory and take and save pictures of the items as they were when they were put in storage.

17. **Separate it.** Especially if you are using long-term self-storage, make a diagram of what you placed where in your storage unit. This could save you time and headaches later on, especially if you need to retrieve certain items. Anticipate items you may need first like seasonal clothes, or shelving, or specific furniture. Make sure these items are last in and can be picked up first easily.

18. **Stacking order.** Place heavier items on the floor and stack them, heaviest to lightest, from bottom to top. Fragile items should be placed on top but be sure they're stable and won't fall over.

19. **Stacking clear.** Be aware of the doorway and avoid overfilling the unit in the area around the doorway. I have seen nightmare situations where people stack high right in the path where the doorway rolls up. They pull the door down to close it, not knowing an item on top was now knocked forward. Then, months later, it is impossible to open and roll the door up because items have fallen forward onto the door.

> "I'm a New Yorker; my oven is used for storage."
>
> —Cheyenne Jackson

THE CONCLUSION

According to statista.com the value of the self-storage market worldwide is over USD 58 billion. In America we are obsessed with our stuff. We place value on our things by attaching memories to them. In some ways I would argue we could say that storage units have become the new Egyptian sarcophagi. We put stuff in them to know that we still have those items even when we do not use them for years at a time. Of course, storage under many applications has an extremely important purpose. I think it is safe to say that the amount of storage we have far surpasses the reasons for necessity. It is who we are as humans.

STORAGE

BONUS TIP: When placing items in storage, fill any hollow spaces, such as shelves, with items. Make sure the shelves can bear the weight of the things you place on them so you don't encounter any unpleasant surprises when you unload the unit.

CLEAN-OUTS AND JUNK REMOVAL

"There is no such thing as "Away." When we throw something away it must go somewhere."

—Annie Leonard

CHECKING IT TWICE

My team was working in 20° weather and struggling through a foot of recently fallen snow. We were cleaning out a home in the famous Hamptons, on Long Island. The property had to be completely "walk through" ready for closing. This included the yard and garages. The issue was that the snow was fresh and then frozen hard. We literally could not shovel it. We could only step down into the snow, spanning long unfamiliar yard and driveway paths. This was difficult at best, almost impossible at worst. When we were wrapping up this long cold winter workday one of the last actions we had to trek through a long distance of snow to load up two BBQ grills. It is important for everyone to know that propane tanks or any flammable gas is not allowed to be transported in commercial trucks. Trucks must be licensed specifically for transporting these dangerous gases. This may not make much sense to the average person. Often people ask us why they have to move their propane tanks to their new home. Why wouldn't trucks be able to take propane? After all, most people take their own propane tanks to the local store in their cars to get them refilled. This is commonplace and often a key indicator of summer grilling season for many.

Welp! This scary story is exactly why trucks are not allowed, and should not be permitted, to transport propane. Two employees and

CLEAN-OUTS AND JUNK REMOVAL

I carried the first BBQ grill through the snow to the truck. We lifted the cover grill with great difficulty as it was almost fully frozen to the BBQ. Once the cover was off, we removed the propane tank and placed it on the side of the garage. I strapped the grill to the truck while my employees went back and retrieved the other one. When they got to the rear of the truck I asked if they had removed the propane tank and they said yes. One of them proceeded to walk back to where he left it and brought it to the side of the garage. His partner started lamenting to me about how hard it was to get out because this cover was even more frozen than the first. This conversation prompted me to try to remove the cover myself. We both pulled and tore on it to no avail. As I surrendered to removing the cover I knelt down and looked under the tarp to make sure the propane tank was in fact removed. Perhaps you could say that double-checking was my OCD. For it was clear in the distance my other employee was carrying a heavy propane tank towards the garage. I confirmed we were clear when I spotted the propane connector dangling under the grill and proceeded to strap it into the truck.

There were five of us split between two trucks and we were two hours from our base all the way in the Hamptons on Long Island. Don't ask me why Long Islanders say we are *in* one place but when it comes to Long Island we say *on*; that's for a different story. We locked up the house, put the key in the lockbox and hurried our mini caravan back to base. I was driving a small dump truck with one employee following behind a large moving box truck with the other three employees. The Hamptons is a famous and crowded place but not in the winter. In the winter it becomes a ghost town for miles and miles. Very few businesses are open and there are not many people around. As we drove mile after mile back to the Long Island Expressway, I remember vaguely seeing smoke in front of me. I didn't think much of it. The day was cold and gray and I was easily mistaking snow drifting in the air for faint smoke. About a minute after I had this thought my guy sitting next to me started up in hysterics. He had been close to napping slouched in the passenger seat and out of nowhere he was in full alert mode screaming asking me why I wasn't reacting to what I was looking at right in front of my face. We honked, called and alerted our other driver to pull over with us. Ten minutes later the five of us just stood in the frozen snow, completely bewildered as to how our entire truck was on fire. We stood in the middle of nowhere as the local fire truck put out the fire before it reached the engine and cab. Our entire back of the truck—the "body or box" was engulfed in flames and we did not have a clue how the fire started. The firemen left, not knowing how as well. We all jumped in the box which had melt marks everywhere and searched for a cause. As we examined the interior, one employee who loaded the second BBQ grill joked as he now effortlessly went to remove the cover which had thawed completely from the fire. As he pulled it up, we all started yelling; the grill had TWO propane tanks, one on each side! The tank we did not know about must have sparked from the vibrations of the truck driving and started a fire. Wow. These grills are really dangerous! To this day we make sure we triple, not double check, all BBQ's.

CLEAN-OUTS AND JUNK REMOVAL

THE ADVICE

You Can't Take It with You When You Die

Everything you own might as well be garbage. Is this harsh? Yes, but here is why. Financially strapped children will actually pay a junk removal company thousands of dollars after you pass away in order to get their inheritance from your home faster. I have seen it and I understand it. This is especially true in the circumstance where your children need the inheritance and a cash buyer with a time constraint comes knocking. Or when the estate has no liquidity or life insurance.

While alive everything you own is of heightened value. This is due to a number of factors. Most important is the memories you attach to your things. The feeling upon purchasing the item. The hard work you put in to be able to afford it. The day you were at the store with a beloved friend or family member. Perhaps the conversations you had about the item, or while using the item with someone who is now deceased. The list goes on.

Yes this is a generalization and the truth is much more complex. Items definitely have value and people will go to great lengths after a parent passes to sell, auction, or consign items in order to get the most value out of them. Also, family members will hold onto certain items that they deem sentimental due to memories they have attached to your items, to honor you. Of course all this is true as well. The point is that under most circumstances the items need to find homes and fast. Or else they wind up in the hands of a junk removal company. An industry which, goloadup.com states, "According to the Bureau of Labor Statistics, the waste management and junk removal sector brings in over $10 billion annually in the United States alone, with a market value of over $1 trillion worldwide."

Along with estates, everyday moves as well as rental properties also have move-out rules; different communities have different requirements for how the home should be left: what items need to stay, and what items must go. Look toward the following Real-World Hacks to help navigate this process.

> "Simplicity boils down to two things: Identify the essential, and eliminate the rest."
>
> – Leo Babauta

THE REAL-WORLD HACKS

1. **Pre-stepping.** Before doing anything get everyone with any claim to items into the house and deadline what they want and do not want. Make sure nothing is left in the house come the day of the cleanout.

2. **Keeping costs down.** If you're retaining a company to make the property closing-ready, get a flat-rate, worst-case scenario cleanout price; if there's a sale to be held, it should be presale worst-case scenario. Provide the closing date up front so everyone is clear on timing. Then determine the best course of action in ridding your home of the unwanted items, whether that means giving them away to family and friends or holding an estate sale. The less that remains for the final cleanout, the lower your cost. After the estate sale, or when you have finished giving away items, get an updated, flat-rate price. If there's an estate sale and somebody is trying to save money,

CLEAN-OUTS AND JUNK REMOVAL

if time is not of the essence, ask if the cleanout company can return at the end of the sale to provide an updated estimate.

3. **Final disposal.** There are several approaches when it comes to disposing of unwanted items. In some instances, people just want the house cleared out for the transfer of ownership. They don't want to invest the time to sell the contents; they just want to move on. We, along with most companies, take care of whatever can be donated, giving the items to charitable organizations according to clients' instructions, and provide a tax receipt, leaving the home broom-clean.

4. **Time it right.** It's imperative to have the exact time of when you must have everything removed. Junk removal should be last after storage, selling items, and moving. Schedule all services accordingly, making sure to leave a day before the deadline.

5. **No surprises,** *please*. Junk removal companies may charge additional fees for bulky, larger, or heavy items, like furniture. Knowing what you need removed and getting an estimate based on that can save you surprises down the road.

6. **Dump it or truck it?** Find out what vehicle they will use to remove your items. Most common is a box truck, dump truck, dump trailer, or dumpster. Beware dumpsters are also known for damaging driveways.

7. **Dispose responsibly.** Be aware beforehand of any items that are not allowed, such as hazardous waste materials, as well as propane tanks. These can include chemicals, paint, etc. Check with the company before you hire them and know what they will and will not handle.

8. **Clear separation.** In cases where most things in a room stay, flip the process and either remove the unwanted items and label the door, or label the junk item only in said room.

9. **Park it.** Park vehicles out of the way so they don't inadvertently get debris on them during the cleanout process. Ask any neighbors in proximity to move their vehicles so they don't get damaged; let them know as soon as you have scheduled your removal so they're aware of the date(s) in advance. This is especially important if you're doing a post-renovation cleanout.

10. **All yours.** The cleanout should be the absolute last thing you do before the walkthrough. All wanted items should be out of the home the day the company arrives for the cleanout. If they are not, for whatever reason, you should make sure they are cordoned off in a separate room or area, labeled clearly, and acknowledged by the company foreman. As for the items remaining in the house for the new homeowner, they too should be labeled clearly for the company foreman.

11. **Flip it.** The home should be left completely empty and broom-swept for the closing walkthrough. What does this mean? This means the home does not have to be cleaning-company-clean, but just empty of all items and nicely swept. If you imagine taking the property and flipping it upside down in the air, whatever falls to the ground that is not organic (like firewood), or a tool for the new owner (like skylight rods), must be removed.

12. **Common Issues.** Things to watch out for include attic spaces, and staircases. Clearing out attics can often lead to a worker's foot going through the ceiling when stepping from beam to beam. Tight staircases often get scraped when heavy, large furniture is moved through them by junk removal laborers who are not professional movers. Make sure you have a conversation about drywall damage and how it will be rectified if something were to happen. You do not want your closing held up or money in escrow because of a last minute drywall issue.

CLEAN-OUTS AND JUNK REMOVAL

13. **Surprises.** Anticipate any surprises that may come up. I have seen wall units removed only to find out that the carpet installer decades prior never moved it and now there's a weird no carpet outline in the floor. Same with built-in cabinets, desks, dressers and things of that nature. Once removed, you realize you have paint differentiation. All these little idiosyncrasies can cause headaches during a walk through.

THE CONCLUSION

If you're waking up in the middle of the night panicking, believe me, I get it. The most important step is knowing that you almost definitely need to clean out your residence and leave it empty and swept. If you are cleaning out junk in order to list a house then I would recommend having a maid service come in after the cleanout. This is also a good idea for those who want to go the extra mile for the people moving into their house. The cleanout company will get you to contract approva, but the house will not be maid service clean by any means. The most important items at this step are knowing that you will need it, knowing what stays for the new owner, removing all items you want, and planning the time just before closing to have the cleanout completed.

BONUS TIP: Renting a dumpster and doing the cleanout yourself may not save you the kind of money you might expect. Typically, it's only 20% to 30% less costly than hiring a company to do it for you, once you account for laborers, dumpsters, tools, etc.

TEMP MOVES
(RESTORATION & RENOVATION)

"If you pay attention to the present, you can improve upon it. And, if you improve on the present, what comes later will also be better."

—Paulo Coelho, The Alchemist

Asbestos Nightmare

A client hired us to move him into his new home. It was a gorgeous $1.5 million home he had bought from a contractor. Flip homes can be dangerous. I have known that from first hand experience. My first home was a starter flip home and it had a shower in the basement that was installed upside down. Something you would never catch on an inspection; it took me showering and the soap dropping to the floor to realize the blunder.

This client's home looked to be top notch. It was a beautiful home on over an acre of property. So I was dumbfounded when the client called me to hire my crew to move all his furniture off his wood floors only one year later. For some reason all of his floors had started to buckle. The house was a ranch and the flooring went throughout the entire first floor of the home. We moved everything off the floors and into the garage and basement. The following day the flooring company pulled up one board and saw asbestos. There are strict laws about asbestos; once a company finds it, they have to stop and call in a professional. The costs for asbestos removal can be astronomical. My client called his insurance company and found out the hard way that there was zero liability for his insurance company because it was done illegally by the construction company that installed the flooring.

Being that the house was recently redone it was easily proven that the contractor had glued the flooring to what was now open and wet asbestos, which is highly illegal. It's okay to have asbestos if it's covered in your house but as soon as there's an open area, that's it, it must be removed. My client was stressed that he had to replace his new floor one year after buying his dream home. Now the stress was about to tsunami through his home as the story continued to unfold. No part of this job was covered, and he was left to foot the bill to remove all the asbestos, which was over $150,000. His only recourse was to go after the construction company, which was obviously liable. He did not know who the construction company was because the last owner hired them. They were long gone by the time he first saw the house. The homeowner who sold the house could just say he did not know he hired a company to renovate it. It could be possible to track down the company and sue, but at what cost? When will the nightmare end?

The Personal Aside

While I was working on this chapter, I was reminded of a story from my past. About six months after I started Relocators in April of 2009, I delivered a speech in front of Archbishop Dolan; Nicholas Scoppetta, the FDNY Commissioner; the fire department's top brass; and about 700 people at the Hilton in New York City. The occasion for the speech was my father receiving the Man of the Year award, bestowed by the Holy Name Society in New York City.

My father worked light duty in the New York City Fire Department (FDNY) Counseling Service Unit (CSU) in the late nineties. He had been asked many times to join the FDNY CSU. He refused because, in effect, to join would mean he could no longer be a fireman. You see, you cannot have a light-duty and a full-duty position at the same time. However, the leaders of the counseling unit pushed, and my dad was granted a rare opportunity to both work in his firehouse fighting fires two nights a week, and in the CSU two days a week. The deal was made and his official start date was September 10, 2001. Somebody put him right where he was supposed to be at the exact moment he was supposed to be there.

For the next 8-plus years, my father worked, saving thousands of heroes' lives. However, he would never admit to this and I never understood why. While writing this chapter, I went on a 12-day retreat with him. On the 13-hour drive back from North Carolina, I asked him about the circumstances of a specific night I remembered where people kept calling to thank him because he saved a fireman's life. The gentleman was a hero fireman in his own right and he was in trouble. He could not be found and his coworkers and friends were getting worried. The conundrum was that they didn't want to make public the fact that the man was missing for an entire day already. Obviously all logical reasoning would say that keeping someone's disappearance a secret is the antithesis to finding him. My dad offered an out-of-the-box idea that resulted in the man being found and brought to safety within that same evening. My father blew off the accolades he'd received and any mention of helping the guy. When I asked why, in a rare, raw moment, he responded, "Because firemen save lives every day, Rob. It's their job." At that moment a concept hit me.

What my father meant was how negligible it was to save a hero who spends everyday saving people's lives himself. He did not want credit or thanks ever. But when I heard what he said I thought something completely different.

From my earliest memories, I remember everywhere I went with my father, someone would say hello to him, then reach for my hand and uncomfortably praise my father by continuously telling me how great he is. I would be in random places, whether it was around his firehouse in Harlem, or a random gyro house late at night in Queens. This happened anywhere we went and it happened often. I would even say when you're that young, around seven or eight years old, everything is normal because you do not know any better. I knew though, even back then, that this was not normal.

So, with my father's response, I made sense of all of that. I also understood why in 2009, he received the Man of the Year Award. It was because firemen save lives every day, and after 9/11 my father, his best friend John Farina, and a few of his nut job friends down at the CSU, were out there saving firemen. Even Superman needs a hero.

At that moment, I remembered a story from the ceremony. Captain Jack Houlihan had spoken just before me. In his speech, Jack told a story where my dad was the chauffeur; his job was to drive the fire truck and connect the water to the hydrant. His captain came down from a brutal fire and happened to see my dad talking to a young lady. He was planning on joking with my father and saying, "We're up there getting our brains blown in and you're down here with a young lady." As the captain got closer, he realized the woman was in hysterics because her apartment had just been destroyed and my dad was consoling her. As he approached, my father turned, saw him, and said, "Damn, Captain, that looked bad from the street. I was saying Hail Marys for you guys." Then he said, "From my angle, the Chief looked like he took a beating. Someone needs to go check on him." It turned out my father was right and the Chief needed to go to the hospital. My dad always watched everything and everyone. The very next day, my dad took off work and spent the day removing the young girl's items that hadn't been destroyed. I say it all the time, but to say it again: moving our things, strangers touching our things, losing all our things, can be challenging and emotional.

But when you step back and really look at it, you'll see that there is so much more going on in life than meets the eye. Life has a way of sewing together major losses and major wins, as all events become lessons in our lives or preparations for future occurrences. Although I heard the story in 2009, I would swear in all honesty that my father absolutely never moved people after fires. Although a major part of my career is dedicated to helping people move after fire and water damage, I always assumed it to be random how I fell into this line of work. I had zero knowledge of any preparation for it, or an understanding of how I could have been influenced into this line of work. Yet when I step back, I can see that hearing Captain Jack's speech probably planted a seed that exploded years later, after I had forgotten it was sown.

> "You can't connect the dots looking forward. You can only connect them looking backward. So you have to trust that the dots will somehow connect in your future. You have to trust in something—your gut, destiny, life, karma, whatever. Because believing that the dots will connect down the road will give you the confidence to follow your heart, even when it leads you off the well-worn path. And that will make all the difference."
>
> —Steve Jobs

TEMP MOVES (RESTORATION & RENOVATION)

THE ADVICE

When you spot damage in your home, before you do anything, call somebody with experience before you call your insurance company. Call a restoration company, call a friend who's familiar with the restoration business. Call a public adjuster whose job it is to advocate for the homeowner. You want someone to advocate for you who has experience. The exception to this is the higher-end insurance companies. If you pay a premium for one of the top-tier insurance carriers, you are in luck. The adjusters advocate for clients, and although the premiums are multiples greater than lower-end carriers; the people you deal with really have your best interests.

There's nothing worse than having to move because of a restoration job. Consider it: when you take an already-stressful event like moving and compound it with damage in your home, it's a complete and utter stress-filled nightmare. Most people who have restoration packouts don't have as much involvement as they would in a typical move. And rightfully so; the stuff coming out of the house is going right back into the same place, which is why it's important to hire a mover yourself, or a restoration company that brings a professional mover. The mover should ideally take an extensive inventory of everything and do a virtual tour of your house, which is easy to set up.

Beware of restoration companies whose staff is doing your packout. For a moving company, obtaining a license to move household goods is fairly difficult to obtain. The license requirements vary in each state, but some like New York are very difficult. The insurance policy itself has multiple parts to it. When damage occur, there are different categories to cover different areas of the damage. Among these are mitigation, reconstruction, and content manipulation, to name a few. The key here is content manipulation. Under the guise of content manipulation, some restoration companies bill insurance companies to move household items. Often this happens in suburban areas. In the suburbs there is more space, which enables restoration laborers to order portable storage containers and fill them with household furniture themselves. I would argue this is not acceptable, but it is definitely a gray area. However, nobody should be moving anything in a truck and putting it in storage unless they're a licensed household goods moving company. So make sure that is the case if you ever find yourself in this position.

THE REAL-WORLD HACKS: RESTORATION & RENOVATIONS

1. **Know who's doing what.** Find out who's handling the move. If you have high-end contents, make sure the people who are moving are from a professional moving company and not workers at the restoration company. If the restoration company staff is doing the moving, ask to see a moving license. They won't have one. Technically, they probably shouldn't. If the belongings are moved on site into portable storage containers, for example, then that may be okay. But restoration company staff should not be manipulating contents to place them on trucks and take them from one location to another.

2. **Document it.** Take detailed pictures of everything, preferably before anybody's in your home doing any work. For photo inventorying, do this yourself before any service professionals come in. It's important to have a photo inventory of all the damaged and potentially damaged areas. The photos should show where everything was when the damage occurred.

3. **Inventory it.** Keep a diligent inventory of the items the carrier adjuster deems lost—the items they're going to reimburse you for. Then also have a detailed inventory of the items that are salvageable, which you won't be getting money for, that are going to storage.

4. **Cleaning costs.** Dry cleaners are going to race to take all your clothing, fabrics, and soft goods to a dry cleaner immediately. Some charge exorbitant amounts of money to insurance companies for this service. Choose dry cleaners wisely. Be involved with your dry cleaner and discuss your options with them. Don't let your insurance company get billed and run up money, especially if you have insurance limits and you can use the money elsewhere. This is especially true for shirts and items you haven't worn in 30 years that were exposed to smoke; cleaning of these is unnecessary in most cases.

We all have clothing we don't care about that's better to throw out than to pay to have cleaned.

5. **Retain or store?** Be diligent about what goes into your temporary living space and what goes into storage. Ensure that you can readily access seasonal clothing and any other items you might need, beyond the time frame the construction estimate provides.

6. **Choose wisely.** Choose your contractors and service providers wisely, keeping costs in mind, especially if you have insurance limits. Have a step-by-step action plan in place that takes all costs into account from the beginning to the end of the restoration process. Make sure you have all items accounted for in the beginning to avoid adding costs to the process.

7. **Cleaning before move-in.** In what's called post-construction cleaning, when a contractor is wrapping up the reconstruction, they send in a cleaning crew to make the home pristine. Make sure the cleaning crew comes in before the movers do. Often people are rushed out of temporary living due to costs and the return move suffers. When cleaners are not finished, the return move becomes fragmented and also the items are in the home while there is still construction dust.

8. **Baby bathwater.** If you leave home in haste due to damage, make sure you go back immediately to retrieve all your personal belongings. Jewelry, money, precious items, important documents, should all be removed by the homeowner and brought to a safe location.

9. **Believe nothing.** I cannot stress this enough: do not believe time frames. Make sure you prepare for the seasons ahead of your estimated completion date.

10. **Zen den.** Plan ways prior to coping with unforeseen stressors that may come up. Construction in a home is known to break up families. Have a plan to stay united when the going gets rough.

TEMP MOVES (RESTORATION & RENOVATION)

11. **Blessing in disguise.** If you're forced to live with aging parents and in-laws during a home remodel, try to find the good in the situation when they are stressing you out. Be thankful they will have added quality time with your children. Know that one day, you may look back and treasure this experience that, today, may seem like torture.

12. **Save on storage.** When possible, if contractors allow, store furniture and non-high-value items in locked rooms or garages that will not be affected by the construction. Send as little as possible to storage.

13. **Finishes before starting.** Plan finishes before beginning any part of the process. If you can, plan the renovation and purchase your finishes, like tiles, cabinets, flooring, siding, countertops, sinks, windows, etc., prior to starting the job. Doing this may save you a lot of money or time in the long run. This is one case where I would recommend renting plenty of storage space. One of the leading causes of construction delays is not having what is needed at the time it is needed. By avoiding this pitfall, you improve your chances of staying on deadline and in the long run, save time and money and, if nothing else, a whole lot of stress.

14. **Mark your territory.** Find something special to do with family, like writing your names in a hidden cement post at the edge of a deck or signing your names and the year on a stud prior to the sheetrock installation. These little markers help bring the whole family together and get them excited about the project. They also create fond memories and are a way to make a time capsule for the future.

15. **Finished topping.** When the move is nearing completion, make sure to photo document the home just before the movers arrive. Urge your moving supervisor to take all proper precautions to ensure none of the freshly done walls or floors are damaged. Precautions could be floor mats, masonite, stair landing covers, wall covers, door jam covers, etc to name a few.

THE CONCLUSION

There are a lot of restoration tricks that can help save you money. If you have a home with wooden floors throughout the entire house, like the client I mentioned at the beginning of this chapter, if there's water damage in one room, you can't match the flooring. You are required to replace the entire floor. However, if you put in a saddle, and you're okay with having that between rooms, you can, in effect, save by not having to replace the entire wood floor, but you only need to replace the flooring in one room. Whether it is a home renovation or a restoration reconstruction, make sure you are purchasing quality materials that will last you. Companies may try to increase profits by purchasing lower quality aftermarket materials, cheaper paint than you had, or lower-quality plywood or sheetrock. Make sure you are involved in what you are getting on the inside as well as the outside of the walls. Construction is hard and long and there's a lot involved. I must stress preparing clothes, toys, and belongings, for one full season past your expected completion date.

> **BONUS TIP:** When purchasing insurance, be vigilant about what is and isn't covered. Saving money is great but sometimes cheap is expensive and expensive is cheap. Make sure you disclose all information about the property to your insurance broker. Even items like trampolines can be important factors in determining types of coverage. The reality is insurance policies are *not* created equally. In the event of a real disaster, you do not want to find out that you saved a couple thousand dollars a year but lost hundreds of thousands due to lack of coverage.

THE EXPERT

Vice President – SERVPRO Team Kluger

Dan Kluger

As a property restoration professional and vice president of SERVPRO Team Kluger serving the New York and New Jersey areas and beyond, our team understands the intricacies and challenges that come with transitions. While our service area spans across the tri-state region, SERVPRO stands as a trusted national resource, ready to deliver exceptional service and support in any crisis that may arise during your move.

When moving, especially into an older or previously occupied property, it's essential to approach the process with a keen eye and proactive mindset. As a SERVPRO professional, I recommend starting with a thorough property inspection, looking for signs of water damage, mold, or structural issues that could escalate if left unaddressed. Pay special attention to visible water damage, suspected mold, and other environmentally hazardous materials that may contain asbestos and lead-based paint. Identifying and addressing these concerns early on can prevent significant health risks and costly repairs in the future.

In the event that mold or water damage is found, it is important that a trained professional restoration contractor specializing in identifying the source of the loss works alongside the homeowners and their insurance agent, broker, or adjuster. SERVPRO is a trusted source for all things property restoration, so whether you have a mold issue in the basement or water damage to the interior, our team is always here to help support movers with flexible solutions.

Additionally, I can recommend these specific services our team members have encountered helping customers during moving situations: (1) Utilize moisture mapping technology to uncover hidden dampness that may elude visual detection. (2) Scheduling professional cleaning services ensures a fresh start by eliminating potential allergens and lingering contaminants. It's also crucial to (3) document everything meticulously—take detailed photos of valuable items and note any existing damage to furniture or appliances. These records are invaluable for insurance claims and future reference. By embracing these proactive measures and leveraging SERVPRO's expertise, you can facilitate a smoother, safer transition into your new property.

"Moving involves more than just boxes and logistics—it's about safeguarding your new beginning. Trust SERVPRO to make your transition smoother and safer, no matter where you move."

10 MILITARY MOVES

"I thank God for my life, And for the stars and stripes. May freedom forever fly. Let it ring, Salute the ones who died. The ones that give their lives. So we don't have to sacrifice. All the things we love"

—Chicken Fried, Wyatt Durrette / Zac Brown

The Story - From An Expert

It's December 1987 and I'm on my way to New York from Hawaii to get married. Being in the military and stationed in Hawaii was a dream but it was about to become a nightmare! Moving myself around is one thing, but what happened over the next 5 years with military moving was certainly something I've never experienced nor ever want to do again. After a brief two-week stay in New York after getting married, it was time to head back to Hawaii, but this time with a wife and all our belongings. Grant it, the Army pays for everything, but we all know about government spending right?!

Well, we contacted the Army moving office and they assigned us a company to come and pick up our belongings. We got our date for pick up and we knew as an overseas client it would take some time, but what happened next we were not ready for. Upon the arrival of the movers, we were told not to pack our own boxes—that they do it all, and the Army already paid for it.

So we sat back and let them do their job and when the truck left, we boarded our flight, carrying only our personal stuff that we didn't want to go without. They told us we should have our stuff in Hawaii in about 10 days. Sounds good,, right? Well almost a month went by and we still didn't have anything, nor did we get any answers. It turns

MILITARY MOVES

out the government uses many different companies to move soldiers, and their belongings all go to different depots and gets stored until they get a space on a ship to transport them. It took almost 3 months to get to us and only half made it. All boxes were trampled, some were opened, and the rest lost. Lifelong memories gone, with some broken items. The Army gave us a check for all the missing and damaged items which were all inventoried by stickers. It was 1987. No barcodes. After 2 years it was time to leave Hawaii and go to Fort Drum, New York. You would think it can never happen twice, right? Well, same process again and same results.

Two months later we got our boxes of broken items and half our belongings, but this time with a twist. None of it was packed in bubble wrap or any protection. We had to leave before the movers came, since we were the verge of Desert Storm and I had to go. My wife was going to go to her family in New York, as we knew I'd be gone for a long time. When I came back, we had to move again, this time to Fort Bragg, and I was determined to make sure that the previous 2 moves would not get repeated. Well, I lost at that as well.

The story is the same, and you can just change the year. All missing and a lot broken. The military has no business moving its people, I feel. Fast forward almost 30 years later and we moved to North Carolina from New York and found that great (not good) movers *do* exist. Rob personally came to the house, looked at everythin, and knew what the cost would be and described step-by-step how it would take place. A team of men came 2 days prior and literally hand-packed everything perfectly.

Rob encountered a problem which was out of his hands reminiscent of my past experiences. The difference was that this time Rob and his team were accountable, transparent and constantly communicating, and effective at rectifying the issue. When the trucks arrived, it was a seamless process to the pull away. We got our trucks to North Carolina to the new house, and couldn't believe the difference. Military moving is still the same way as I hear from friends still in the service and even their kids. They should take lessons from this book Rob is writing because he does it right!

Mike Scialabba

Owner East End Helicopter LLC

EastEndHelicopter.com

Veteran US Army

THE ADVICE

The first piece of advice I have is that we all pause for a moment of silence. I'd like to wholeheartedly thank Mike Scialabba, along with Lee Zeldin, Former New York Congressman; who also gave a feature located at the end of this chapter, and all the other military personnel who have either risked or given their lives for us to live a life of freedom. Thank you!

Similar to a civilian move, if you're looking at an upcoming move for the military, you can help make the transition easier with a bit of advance planning. Being aware of (and availing yourself of) the options available to you is a good place to start. Below are a few tips to point you in the right direction.

As soon as possible after you receive your Permanent Change of Station (PCS) or Temporary Duty Move (TDY)/Temporary Duty Assignment (TDA) orders, it's a good idea to contact your base transportation management office (TMO) to set up a meeting. One thing you might ask the TMO is to double-check that everyone who is moving with you is included on your orders. This is an important step, because it ensures your family members will be approved to move with you.

When it comes to finances, you can reach out to your family center to find out what relocation assistance is available to you. It's also a good idea to schedule a meeting with the finance office in your current location to find out what your moving options are and what costs, if any, you will be responsible for. You may be entitled to receive reimbursements or allowances (broadly referred to as "entitlements") to help cover your moving costs. If you're responsible for any moving expenses, you may be able to claim them on your tax return.

For PCS moves, you can choose whether you want to do a full or partial DIY move (referred to as a Personally Procured Move or PPM). A list of authorized (reimbursable) and unauthorized expenses is provided for PPMs at dfas.mil. With a full government PCS, the military handles the planning, packing, transport, and unpacking of your belongings; they also cover all of the costs involved with the move.

A sponsor, assigned to you in your new location before you arrive, can assist with any questions you may have, both before and after your relocation. Be prepared with questions to ask your sponsor so they can help you navigate the transfer to your new home.

Most military personnel will be familiar with *https://www.militaryonesource.mil/*. Here you will find extensive information on all that is available to you from the Defense Department to assist with your relocation. This resource seems very thorough and helpful, equipped with everything from being compensated for the move to audio clips explaining all the different parts of moving. While digitally the military seems to have come a long way from Mike's experiences. I hope that to be true in execution as well. My fear, though, is it may not have. Being that the military is government-run, my personal experience with military moves is extremely limited. I will not do soldiers the dishonor of saying I have the answers, either. I am not an expert on military moves, being that they are tied to the government. The hacks here are what I theorize may help, as I attempt to offer any solace possible if I could.

THE REAL-WORLD HACKS

1. **Air tags.** Mike's story immediately brings to mind the importance of air tags and other tiny tracking devices. Luckily, today these items are economical and plentiful. I would put one in every box after hearing Mike's story.

MILITARY MOVES

2. **Home is where the heart is.** Bring a personal memento or picture of loved ones for memory, sanity, and peace. Any little bit of home can help give you comfort while enduring harsh times, I bet.

3. **Reserve-ready.** For reserve members, make sure all utilities, bills, and monthly obligations are in the hands of a trusted family member or friend.

4. **Forward plan.** Have a dependable plan ready for any pets or plants you may have in your home.

5. **Miser among us.** Find ways to save on monthly accounts like cable, phone bills, and utilities to avoid spending money on things you're not using. Month-to-month subscriptions allow you to discontinue services when you're not using them. Digital thermostats that you can control with your smartphone are a way to remotely adjust temperature settings and turn heating and cooling off and on.

6. **Prevent catastrophe.** Make sure utilities are set or scheduled to avoid damage. Be sure to take preventative measures to avoid hoses or pipes freezing during cold weather. In extremely hot weather, paint can sweat and furniture may be damaged.

7. **Retain the essentials.** Set aside anything that the movers shouldn't pack. This includes essential items that you will need to take with you and that you don't want loaded on the moving truck. This may include valuable items, toys for children, and necessities like plates and kitchen utensils, bedding, and clothing. Place these items in a designated area of your home, like a closet, and clearly label them. Be sure to inform the movers of these items when they arrive so they don't mistakenly pack them.

8. **Travel smart.** Schedule your travel arrangements in advance of the move. If you will have time, you may be able to turn your relocation into a vacation for the family.

9. **Mail forwarding.** Set up mail forwarding or, if you're going to an overseas location, consider having your mail put on hold or forwarded to a trusted friend or family member. You can also have mail forwarded to a receiving unit office.

10. **Get organized.** The Stressless PCS Kit (stresslesspcskit.com) is a labeling system to help military families better plan and organize their move. The kit contains labels for boxes, a room chart, instructions, and door hangers. You can also use the color-coding system described in the Real-World Hacks section of Chapter 4.

11. **You do it best.** Take your own inventory. Take your own pics. Make sure you know what is in each box. With military moves especially make sure you are involved in capturing all of your own records.

THE CONCLUSION

There is a stark difference between private industry and government agencies and how they operate. We all have heard or experienced how difficult it could be to work with government agencies; think Department of Motor Vehicles.

Moving is hard under all circumstances. Even when you pay for the absolute best and receive white glove service, the act of moving in itself is still very stressful. Men and women who are the bravest among us deserve the benefits that come with such sacrifices. Unfortunately, the benefit of a complimentary move by a government agency can also lead to a difficult situation being much more difficult than it has to be. This is unfortunate, but sometimes this is the reality. The best thing you can do is protect yourself with planning, record keeping, and be proactive. As I started, I will end. Thank you for your service and the freedoms all of us enjoy because of your sacrifices.

> **BONUS TIP:** For the reserve members and those who have to move temporarily and often: prior to leaving, enlist a close friend or family member to be your entrusted go-to person. In the event something needs to be handled suddenly, it will save you a lot of time not having to decide who you should call from back home to help.

THE EXPERT

–Lee Zeldin, Administrator of the U.S. EPA

"It is important to photograph your belongings just before the move, make sure the inventory is accurate, inspect your property quickly on the other end of the move, and file claims for damage promptly afterwards. Bring any items with you that you can that are especially important to you and that you don't want damaged or destroyed."

BUSINESS MOVES

"Appearing better than others is always dangerous, but most dangerous of all is to appear to have no faults or weaknesses. Envy creates silent enemies. It is smart to occasionally display defects, and admit to harmless vices, in order to deflect envy and appear more human and approachable. Only gods and the dead can seem perfect with impunity."

"There is nothing more intoxicating than victory, and nothing more dangerous."

"Despise the free lunch."

—Robert Greene, *The 48 Laws of Power*

WHIMS OF THE MAN

One of my clients, an accountant, needed to move his firm of 43 associates. By nature, accountants are analytical, great planners, and cautious. This accountant called us four separate times over the course of a year for estimates. In the meetings, we developed a great rapport with each other, but I could not figure out if he was just price-shopping or being overcautious to a fault. I came to find out he was actually the victim. He was past his lease and had been renting his office space on a month-to-month basis for years. His landlord refused to sign another lease with him because he was unsure what his plan was with the building as a whole.

For estimate #1, we were moving him to another floor in the building and he was signing an extended lease with the landlord. For estimate #2, he was looking for a new building because his landlord had decided to sell the building and he was unsure if the new landlord would keep him and, if so, at what rate per square foot. For estimate #3, a major corporation had bought the building and he was sure he would have to move out immediately. Then for estimate #4, COVID hit, the major corporation backed out and, although a new buyer went into contract, the accountant now had half of his associates working from home. Extremely frustrating, especially for someone who is a disciplined thought-out planner by instinct. Now, he had to make a decision and the new landlord was pushing him into a long-term lease. At this point he had stability from the building decision makers and non-stability within his own organization.

Because he was unsure of the space he needed, he did not want to sign the lease. He opted for a new building where he would have less space but the flexibility to take on more space if he needed it in the future. He also put all of his extra equipment and furniture in storage. The new landlord was more flexible with options and more secure with his plans for occupying the building long-term. The moral of the story is when we think of the nightmare of moving, the crazy part is that the nightmare does not just take place on moving day. It's all the things that happen long before, and sometimes until long after, moving day.

THE ADVICE

Whether you're moving because your company is downsizing or it's bursting at the seams, business moves can be complex. When moving a company, you're not just moving you and your family, you are moving everyone. Next to home, work is where most people spend most of their time. So moving work is a big deal for everyone, not just the business owner. In either of these scenarios, planning ahead and getting as organized as possible before the move can mean a more seamless transition.

In business, knowing when to, or why to, move can be a challenge. It's important to identify the reasons to move your business as well as to be able to anticipate the needs of your business. It's also helpful if you can move on your own terms. If you have a store, is there a better location that has become available? If you're going to be adding a new department, for example, how many offices will you need and how well will your current space accommodate the expansion? Or maybe you're at the other end of the spectrum: you've restructured the business and you're now paying for empty space.

If you feel that your business would benefit from professional advice, operational efficiency experts and business consultants are very common. These professionals focus on helping businesses improve their operations and optimize growth. My advice for hiring these professions is to find them from a trusted referral source. Perhaps a local networking group or social media business group can offer dependable referrals. Ultimately the best advice givers are those who have actually done it and are consulting from experience. Experience and a client testimonial are the two main things you should look for when vetting people.

Purchasing commercial property is a different ball-game when compared to purchasing residential property. I have purchased commercial property more than a few times and each time I learned something unique. For instance, commercial property signs are often used by commercial realtors as a way of gaining clients, and will usually be kept up long after the property has been rented or sold so that the people interested become clients of the property agent. Commercial leases differ from residential leases. Often equipment such as AC units or heating systems are the responsibility of the tenant, which is not the case with residential leases. Property taxes are usually divided up and paid by tenants in commercial leases.

Assessing the environmental condition before you purchase a property is very important, and knowing the past owners and uses of the property can be a good indicator of possible environmental problems. Chemicals can seep into the ground of commercial facilities occupied by industries like manufacturing, toxic-level painting, auto body shops, and auto mechanics; to name a few. Environmental professionals provide an investigation to determine the presence of contaminants on the property.

Much like residential property inspections, the buyer foots the bill for these reports. Depending on which company you hire, environmental reports may be completed in a few phases and can include a record search that often includes a risk assessment. The investigation typically examines nearby properties as well. If there is reason to believe that the property you're considering buying is contaminated, additional tests will analyze the quality of the air, groundwater, and soil. Soil samples are a lower cost early phase to detect any contamination in the ground. These are extremely important because, in the event there is contamination, once purchased, the buyer of the property is responsible for the costs of remediation and environmental cleanup, even if they didn't cause the contamination.

If you'll be leasing a space, be sure to carefully review the contract before signing it to make sure you're aware of any expenses and expectations (such as for maintenance) that are associated with the property. Pay attention to any responsibilities you'll have for things like taxes, insurance, and other incidental costs. Working with expert commercial real estate lawyers and advisors is paramount for both leasing and purchasing.

When it comes to financing, the 504 loan program is a difficult loan to get, but if you qualify it is a great tool for business owners looking to purchase property. The loan provides long term, fixed-rate financing for major fixed assets, such as equipment or real estate. The loan comes with a criteria that involves job growth, loan use, and revenue parameters. Regular commercial loans typically require more than 20% down payment. They also have short terms as low as five years with longer amortization periods, meaning every five years you must refinance, which exposes you to interest rate changes multiple times over the course of a property loan lifecycle. The 504 loan is the federal government partnered with a bank, and the term of the loan is usually much longer. The 504 loan I have has a twenty-year term with a thirty year amortization. This offers much more security than my other commercial loans, which are five-year terms with twenty year amortization.

THE REAL-WORLD HACKS

1. **Be prepared.** Give yourself plenty of time to plan and prepare for the move. Start boxing up items, purging unnecessary files and equipment, and taking apart furniture well ahead of time. This will also save money and time, as a big part of moving costs is labor.

2. **Designate a coordinator.** Assign a project manager to coordinate the transition and generally keep things on track. This person should handle all aspects of the move and filter all communications between the company you hire, management, employees, and vendors.

3. **Plan for growth.** The new location should take into account both your business's current size and its projected expansion.

4. **Items in stock.** Make sure you have plenty of inventory to see the business through the move and a bit beyond. Keep in mind how long you will need to unpack everything.

5. **Plan to be delayed.** Build more time than you think you need into the transition timeline to account for unexpected delays. This cushion of time, along with advance planning and preparation, can help reduce stress and make things go more smoothly.

6. **Everyone on the same page.** Communicate with key personnel, employees, and service providers throughout the transition to ensure everyone is aware of things like changes to the plan or timeline, what is happening and when, and who is responsible for what. Also make sure you communicate with customers at key intervals to let them know of the upcoming move and when you'll be open for business.

7. **Timing is everything.** Time the move to minimize the impact on the business. This is especially important for seasonal businesses.

8. **Address change notifications.** Contact other business entities—like the IRS, financial institutions, officials in charge of zoning, the Secretary of State, utilities providers, and service providers—to notify them of your change of location. Be sure to set up mail forwarding and post your new address on your website and social media at the relevant times.

9. **Market it.** Where suited, consider hosting a sale or other event celebrating your move to bring people into your new location.

10. **Mind the technicalities.** Keep in mind that some office equipment, like copiers, may require that certain licensed service professionals move it. Coordinate the relocation of office equipment—everything from servers to printers—with the IT team in advance and work with them to set a timeline.

11. **Hire the best.** Find a reputable mover that specializes in business and commercial moves. Just as you would do before hiring any professional, read their reviews and research their online presence. If you have cubicles make sure they are knowledgeable about taking them apart.

12. **Technology first.** Set up office equipment in the new location before everything else is moved, including servers, phones, internet, computers, and all other equipment.

13. **Inside scoop.** Talk to other businesses in the place you're moving to. They often can tell you all the ins and outs of the area. What are the best vendors to use? Where are the best parking areas? What happens on a weekly basis that you should look out for? When is the garbage picked up? When is the mail delivered?

14. **DIY that.** Make sure all personal items in the business are packed and moved; at the very least, they should be packed by the employees themselves. Things like desk and cubicle contents, photos, and any decorations an employee has in their personal space should be their responsibility to pack and, in some cases, to move. Having them set up their new workspace with their own things is important, both for work and personal reasons, and creates excitement for their new space. Inertia can set in during a move, and more hands make easier work.

15. **Snooki rules.** As Nicole mentions below, make sure all items that need to be set up first are loaded last onto the truck. If placing items in storage, make sure they're separated from the other contents. With business moves, placing items like file cabinets, cubicles, or shelving first is usually imperative.

THE CONCLUSION

I was at dinner with an old friend, John Breazano, or "Breeze" as he is usually called. John is a well-known promotional director whose influence has grown throughout the country. He had been texting with Nicole (Snooki) at dinner. She was talking about her Snooki shop store and how she had to move it from Beacon, New York to Huntington, Long Island. We both just jumped through the conversations without realizing the obvious. Cue in the scene from *Dumb and Dumber*: "Wait, do you want me to tell Nicole you will do her store move?" he asked. "Of course," I replied.

You know that scene in *Dumb and Dumber* when Harry and Lloyd are down-and-out walking down the highway. Then a bus full of Hawaiian Tropic Bikini models pulls over and asks them where they could find two men to come on tour with them to help oil their bodies before competition. Harry and Lloyd assist them by directing them to a town where they could probably find a lot of men willing to do it. They then ponder how some guys are about to get so lucky, and reassure themselves that one day their day,, too will come. Yup, Breeze and I had that moment.

Working with Nicole's staff when we moved her store was a pleasure. They were such a professional organization and my staff had a good time working with them. I went with Breeze to the grand opening and was even more impressed by the staff when I saw them dealing with the crowds and media everywhere. It was cool to have a bird's eye view of her promoting her new business location, as well as the warm welcome the entire town was giving her.

Not all businesses, but in some (I would argue most) the location, be it geographically or structurally, is vital to the success of the company long-term. There are a lot of factors involved in choosing a new location. Some of those considerations include ease of access for customers, parking availability, zoning restrictions, nearby businesses, the condition of the area, and access to shipping and receiving. There should also be enough room for business growth and the space should easily accommodate all office spaces, equipment, and inventory. Ideally, parking should be sufficient to accommodate employees and customers.

I strongly recommend to all business owners, both big, small, and all in between, to treat the decision of their business relocation as seriously as they treat operational decisions, within their business themselves. Whether it is commercial, office, retail, industrial, warehousing, ecommerce, or another, the location or even lack of location for remote companies, is one of the most important factors in industry. All the needs will be different for each type of company but no matter what, *where* the company does business and *how* it is able to operate in that space could determine the success of that company.

> **BONUS TIP:** The commercial real estate industry is different from residential real estate. Something to consider: there are always diamonds in the rough. I have found great success in owning commercial properties. I find that, because there are people who inherit commercial portfolios from a business owner's parents, you often find situations where someone with no interest suddenly owns a lot of properties. If you can, it's always best to hold out for the diamond in the rough.

> **BONUS TIP:** Contact the local chamber of commerce and see if you can have an event or attend a meeting to drum up business in your new location.

BUSINESS MOVES

THE EXPERT

—Nicole LaValle, AKA Snooki

"When moving The Snooki Shop from Beacon, New York to Huntington, New York, having Relocators assist alongside my staff with packing, storing, and unpacking items made going from one location to another all the more effortless. I also found it very helpful when moving store locations to make sure my shelving and racks were packed separately so that when the contractor needed them first, they could be sent to the store without having to do a major search for them in storage."

12
INTERNATIONAL MOVES

"Toto, I've a feeling we're not in Kansas anymore."

—Judy Garland "The Wizard of Oz"

Horse of a different color

At the time of his move into storage one of our clients didn't know that he would be moving to Mexico a year or two later. When he found out, he immediately called us to see if we could help. Help yes, do the move, no. Turns out the help he needed was a lot more than any of us anticipated. Our client hired a third-party container company. Like jobs we do everyday; we assumed we were being hired to load that container to keep his items safe and wrapped professionally. He arranged the container company. He arranged for us to load the containers. He arranged for the trucking company to pick the container up from us and have it at the port for the ship during a specific window of time. Then he received the instructions from customs.

The instructions were unlike anything we were used to or had seen before. Nothing out of our realm but what he needed was multiple times more work than any of us had anticipated. Three truckloads of items had been sitting in storage for over a year. Our plan had been to easily load all the items into the containers and hand over a copy of our inventory to the client. Instead we had to spend the better part of a week prepping his entire shipment. Every single item down to the smallest spoon needed to be unpacked or unwrapped completely. We had to take about four pictures of each item and upload the pictures. Then write the item down on an inventory and add a corresponding letter and number to the item on the inventory sheet. Then we wrote the number on a card in front of the item and uploaded a final picture. We needed to keep a written list inventory that corresponded with the letter and number as well as a printed photo inventory. This had to be done for every item both large and small as well as any large items that had to be taken apart. Not only did we have to repack and rewrap every single item, but the client also had high end art and items in specialty crates we had custom-constructed a year prior. We had to pry all of those open and then remake them from scratch.

THE ADVICE

Sources estimate that more than 8 million Americans live abroad and that 34% of US citizens still living in the States would move overseas if they had the means. There's a lot to be said for exploring new places and experiencing new ways of life, and a lot of people dream of hopping a plane and soaring into new adventures. Oh, if only it were that simple.

By far, one of the most complicated moves you could ever make is an international one. Moving overseas requires a lot of advance planning and an even more amount of research. But, as with anything complex, arming yourself with information is key. Look into things like requirements for immunizations, visa and immigration paperwork, health care, finances, mobile phone plans, driving, housing, shipping, storage, taxes, and more. However, beginning the planning process as far ahead as possible can minimize stress and ensure you're ready to go.

Before applying for a visa, you'll need a current passport. If you don't know when you'll be returning to the US and your passport expires while you're outside of the States, you can renew it at a US embassy. Make sure all important paperwork is kept with you at all times. Have digital copies as well. If you're moving abroad to work or study, be sure to bring proof with you. Some countries also require financial documents to prove you can support yourself while you're there. Ideally, all important documents should travel with you until you're settled in your new residence.

International movers should be licensed and, ideally, they should also have experience moving clients to the specific country you're relocating to—the key being how familiar they are with that country's regulations and restrictions on what items can be imported. Overseas movers should have a FIDI license or be licensed with the Federal Maritime Commission.

When it comes to deciding who to hire, there are several considerations to bear in mind. I recommend following all the advice in the first chapter, "The Art of Selecting a Mover." Along with some more extensive details, you will want to research with international movers. Such as, does the moving company require background checks for the people it hires? And, before you sign on the dotted line, be sure to review the final contract in full and look into any third-party contractors that will be handling your belongings.

Make sure to hire a company that guarantees you one point of contact throughout the move from beginning to end. Pay extra money and request this if you cannot find a company that offers it. In the end it will be well worth it if something were to go wrong. Your items can be shipped by air or sea. Air shipments are the more expensive option but arrive faster. For sea freight, items can be shipped in a separate container or you can share a container with others.

Ask your movers about the cost differences between the two, especially if your belongings won't fill an entire container. Shipping containers are available in 20-ft. and 40-ft. sizes. When shipping by sea freight, a full container load, or FCL, refers to a shipping container used for one client's belongings. FCL costs are billed at a flat rate for use of the entire container. You can also opt for a less than container load (LCL), which means you'll be sharing the container with others. Online sea freight calculators are available to help provide an estimate of how much you can expect to pay for an overseas shipment. The cost depends on the destination and origin countries, the shipping container size, and whether you use LCL or FCL (or air freight).

Border officials require an itemized inventory of everything you're bringing into the country. This helps them to calculate customs duties and monitor goods. It also allows you to make sure you received everything once it's delivered. Be sure to look into what items are allowed in your destination country and which aren't before you ship, as some countries won't allow some seemingly harmless items (for example, you can't bring Kinder Eggs into the US!). Most countries will perform physical inspections of your belongings and scan them by X-ray. The way you pack is also important. The longer it takes for customs officials to sort through your items, the more you will be charged. So pack wisely.

One thing to keep in mind for most international shipments is that the serial number for every electronic item needs to be included in the photographic inventory and on the box. If you don't pack everything or if you miss a box, which happens often in moving—even the best of the best do that—it's practically impossible to re-ship it. But if you don't have serial numbers on the boxes and the customs officials find electronics, know that you will be unpacking everything.

To help pave the way for a smooth transition, it's helpful to research the city you're moving to before you get there. Where will you buy groceries? What entertainment options are available in your area? Will you need to learn a new language? What is the cost of living like, compared to where you currently live? What are the local customs and what do you need to know to avoid inadvertently offending someone? How easy is it to get around?

When it comes to your health, will your current insurance provider cover you in your new location? Some insurance companies offer international health care plans. Depending on where you're going, you may or may not have access to local health care. You may also be required to have certain immunizations to enter the country, so be sure to bring your immunization records, as well as your medical records, with you. If you take prescription medication, is it available in your destination country and if not, is there a suitable replacement for it? Can you bring your current prescriptions with you into the country?

For finances, will you be able to open a bank account in your new location and what is required for you to do this? You may need to establish a certain residency status before you can open a local account. If you can, it could be helpful to maintain your US bank account, especially if you're planning to return. If you can open a local bank account, it eliminates any international transaction fees your bank may charge, not to mention exchange rates that may not work in your favor, especially if you'll be paid in the local currency.

Taxes are another matter. If you live and work abroad as a US citizen, your income is considered foreign-earned, even if a US company is paying you. You're still required to pay US taxes as long as you're a US citizen. But you may meet the qualification requirements for foreign income tax credits and/or foreign earned income exclusion. It's a good idea to consult a tax professional who specializes in expatriate taxes before you leave, to avoid any unpleasant surprises later and to allow you to plan ahead.

International -oves are so complicated and all encompassing. With that being said, although I know it may not always be possible, the best-case scenario is to visit the place you will be moving to prior to actually moving there. Living in the area for even a few days will give you insight into things you may need.

INTERNATIONAL MOVES

THE REAL-WORLD HACKS

1. **Backpacking.** Make sure you can live in the new country for an extended period of time with what you have with you. It can take a long time for your items to arrive through customs. Do not put yourself in a position where you have pressure waiting for important items.

2. **Money matters.** Look at your finances. Make a budget that includes your projected living expenses as well as any current expenses you'll need to cover while you're abroad. It's ideal to have at least 6 months worth of living expenses saved up before you move. This can act as a cushion and at the least, can give you peace of mind during the transition.

3. **Getting your ducks in a row.** Research visa and immunization requirements as far ahead of your move as possible. Some documents, like immigration paperwork, may take several months to process.

4. **Covering your health.** Research health insurance options before you travel. How will you be covered and what are the requirements for you to obtain coverage in your destination country? Some countries have residency requirements you have to meet before you can be insured. Will your current insurance plan cover you while you're abroad?

5. **Rx.** Speaking of health, will you be traveling with medications and are they allowed in the country? If not, are there viable replacement options available?

6. **Money moves.** If your move is a permanent one, look into financial institutions and exchange rates. How will you transfer your money to your new bank and will you need to keep your US bank account open? Having a bank account in the destination country and using

it for transactions in that country will avoid international transaction fees, not to mention unfavorable exchange rates.

7. **Passport applications.** Processing times for a US passport are from 6 to 8 weeks for standard service and 2 to 3 weeks for expedited service. If you need it faster, you can schedule an appointment for urgent service if you have international travel booked within 14 calendar days. The fee increases for the faster processing times, so it's better to apply for or renew your passport as soon as possible. You can also renew your passport at US embassies. The US Embassy offers something called the Smart Traveler Enrollment Program, which provides updates on safety conditions in your destination country.

8. **Education prep.** If you're bringing children, where will they attend school and what are the requirements to get them enrolled?

9. **Pet prep.** If you're traveling with pets, be sure to research your destination country's vaccination requirements ahead of time. As a preventive measure, you might consider microchipping your pets before your trip.

10. **To have on hand.** Bring important documents with you, like birth and marriage certificates, social security cards, immunization paperwork, and your passport. It's also a good idea to have both electronic and original (official) paper copies of these documents on hand.

11. **Staying connected.** While an international phone plan is an option, they tend to be expensive. One option is to ask your carrier to unlock your smartphone and buy a SIM card from a local provider in your destination country.

12. **Nothing is certain but death and taxes.** If you retain US citizenship, you're required to file US taxes, often in addition to filing taxes in your new country. An accountant, ideally one who specializes in

expatriate taxes, can provide information on any tax exemptions you may qualify for.

13. **Mail forwarding.** The USPS will forward mail to an international address, but before you submit this form, it's a good idea to look into the reliability of the mail service in your new area. You can also have mail forwarded to a post office box in the States or sent to a trusted friend or family member.

14. **Fee finding.** Find out whether you'll be charged international transaction fees on purchases made abroad with your credit card. It's also a good idea to find out what the fees will be for any ATM withdrawals you make overseas.

15. **Financial notifications.** Notify your bank and credit card providers before you travel so they know you'll be living abroad and will authorize your transactions.

16. **Talk to the pros.** Consult an immigration professional to ensure you have all of the required documents and paperwork lined up before the move. Immigration experts are also good resources to consult on what is and isn't allowed in the country, which is especially important if you're having anything shipped to you.

17. **Adaptation.** Don't forget to purchase adapters that fit the outlets in your new destination.

18. **Give yourself deadlines.** Make a checklist that includes what needs to be done and when. This should ideally include deadlines for things like visa and passport applications.

19. **Planning ahead.** Overseas shipments should generally be arranged at least 3 to 4 months in advance of the move.

20. **Don't ship that!** What not to have shipped overseas: hazardous materials, medications, firearms, money, alcohol, perishable items, and valuables such as jewelry. Looking into what is and isn't allowed in your new location is always a good idea, as every country has

specific items they do not allow, some of which are seemingly harmless.

21. **Pack for safe transport.** When packing items for overseas shipping, be sure to pack them with extra cushioning, as they may be in for a rough ride.

THE CONCLUSION

I strongly believe that it's important to do things that make you happy. With all the work that goes into a move overseas, doing what makes you smile is even more important. That could mean nights out and planning culinary adventures or outings with your family. But especially if you're traveling alone, meeting other people will help you to establish a sense of connection to your new location and to the community. Joining certain interest groups, like yoga classes or gym centers, can help ease the transition and remind you that you're not alone. It could be fun to be a stranger in a strange land. Enjoy it.

> **BONUS TIP:** For overseas shipments, if you're moving items that need to be crated, like pianos or antique furniture, this will incur additional costs. If you're willing to part with these items and you want to keep costs down, consider selling or leaving them with a trusted friend or family member. Depending on how long you plan to be overseas, storage in the US may also be an option.

INTERNATIONAL MOVES

THE EXPERT

Nicolas Castillo, CPA expert in US Expat Taxes

When Americans move abroad, they often encounter a surprising aspect of US tax rules: any individual who is a US citizen or green card holder must file a tax return no matter where in the world they live. They must report all of their worldwide income to the US and potentially pay US taxes. If they live in a country that has a local tax rate, then they may have to deal with foreign tax systems.

There are a few exceptions for US citizens and green card holders. A single person making less than $12,950 does not need to file a tax return. If you are married and filing jointly, that threshold is doubled. If you are self-employed, earning more than $400, then you have to file a tax return to cover your social tax obligations, which include Social Security and Medicare taxes. Otherwise, if you don't meet any of these thresholds, you are required to report your income and activities.

Another important form to get to know when you move out of the US is related to your foreign financial assets and accounts. The Foreign Account Tax Compliance Act (FATCA) was implemented to combat individuals hiding money in undisclosed offshore accounts. The Foreign Bank Account Report (FBAR) is required if you have more than $10,000 in a non-US account at any point during the year. IRS Form 8938 is triggered if your assets exceed $200,000 as a single person (or $400,000 if married and filing jointly). The thresholds may vary if you have foreign financial assets while living in the United States.

Double taxation is an important concept because most tax rules aim to reduce, if not fully eliminate, it. The US tax code and regulations have provisions such as the Foreign Earned Income Exclusion (FEIE) and the Foreign Tax Credit. The FEIE allows you to exclude up to a certain amount ($120,000 in 2023) of your foreign-earned income from US taxes, provided you meet the residency requirements or the physical presence test. Whether you are working for a US employer, a foreign company, or you are self-employed, as long as you are physically abroad, you may qualify.

The Foreign Tax Credit enables you to claim a dollar-for-dollar credit on taxes paid to a foreign country. For example, if you paid $30,000 to the Australian Taxation Office for your new job in Sydney, you would be able to apply a $30,000 credit against your US tax on the same income.

If double taxation cannot be avoided through either of these methods, we would then look to the tax treaties. The US Government has agreements with several countries to prevent double taxation and simplify cross-border commerce. These treaties can be beneficial in some cases, although not all expats can take advantage of them.

Filing deadlines for US taxes also come with some leniency for expats. While the standard deadline is April 15, Americans living abroad automatically receive a two-month extension to file their returns, moving the deadline to June 15. Americans abroad can request a further extension to October 15, especially if more time is needed to gather local tax information. Note: the extension applies only to the filing date, not the payment date. Any taxes owed should still be paid by April 15 to avoid interest charges. If absolutely necessary, an expat can extend their tax filing to December 15.

If you've fallen behind on your US tax filings as an American living outside the US, the IRS offers the Streamlined Filing Compliance Procedures. This program allows expats who meet certain criteria to catch up on their returns without facing penalties. This is a very valuable option for those who were unaware of their filing obligations or who have inadvertently missed deadlines. For example, someone who was born with American citizenship and has lived outside the US their whole life may not have realized they are required to file. They would be able to file under the streamlined procedures, catching up with just three year's worth of tax returns, and all previous years are forgiven.

Understanding your tax obligations in your host country is equally important. Whether or not you need to file depends on the country and its specific tax laws. Generally, you are considered a resident based on the number of days you spend in the country. Non-residents typically only pay taxes on income earned within the country. For example, in the Bahamas and Kuwait, residents are not subject to income tax, but other taxes like property tax may apply. It's crucial to familiarize yourself with the tax requirements of your host country to ensure you are fully in compliance.

State taxes in the US can also complicate matters. Some states require you to file a state return even if you are outside the US, based on whether you maintain ties to the state, such as property ownership or voter registration. Certain types of income, such as the sale of a home, are considered sourced to the state and may still be subject to state and local tax. The rules vary widely across all 50 states, so understanding the specifics of your home state is essential before moving. For instance, states like California, South Carolina, and New York have stricter requirements, while Florida and Texas are much more lax.

Managing your entire expat tax situation can be cumbersome, but with careful planning and the right resources, you can ensure compliance and optimize your global tax burden. Staying organized with detailed records of your income, expenses, and foreign taxes is essential, as well as paying and filing on time. It may make sense to seek professional help from a tax professional who specializes in expat taxes. They can provide invaluable assistance and peace of mind, guiding you through the nuances of both US and foreign tax systems and helping you make the most of available exclusions, credits, and treaties.

The Chapter After 12th & Before 14th
(Because you will not find a 13th floor in a building elevator, nor should you here.)

MOVING THE ELDERLY

"Remembering that I'll be dead soon is the most important tool I've ever encountered to help me make the big choices in life. Because almost everything—all external expectations, all pride, all fear of embarrassment or failure—these things just fall away in the face of death, leaving only what is truly important."

—Steve Jobs

"Some seniors have Alzheimer's; the rest have half-heimer's. Go easy on them. Old age is a gift many do not receive."

—Robert Esposito

Town Hall Mayhem

Hurricane "Superstorm Sandy" was a major event on Long Island in 2012. When you think of catastrophes in New York in recent history, September 11th and Hurricane Sandy immediately come to mind for most New Yorkers.

Sandy was rough and most of Long Island had no power for over a week or two. Entire towns were flooded and the cost of damage in New York was well over $15 Billion. I was barely a business owner at the time. It had been four years since I started my company and I was still at what I like to call that self-employed stage. Back then the only two services we offered were moving and cleanouts. There was not much moving during the months after the hurricane, so the business survived on the abundance of cleanouts and junk removal that was now needed. One island off the coast of Queens, called Breezy Point, was a summer beach town mostly made up of city police, firemen, and trade union workers. Breezy Point is on a very unique peninsula, and in Breezy Point all the houses are on the beach sand, just feet apart from each other. The entire peninsula would be flooded and destroyed. During the storm, one bridge became impassable. These factors lead to a major domino event when the houses started to catch fire. When you do not have flood insurance, some say the only thing you can do when you're about to lose everything is light a match. Regardless of the rumors or the reasons, basically hundreds of houses burned down while rescue crews could just watch from the other side of the bridge.

At this time I had never even heard of Breezy Point, but that night affected my entire career, company, and every employee that has ever worked at Relocators since. A couple of years later, Breezy Point received a grant to raise all of the houses. Like most Government policies, this help came perfectly after all the houses had been rebuilt and everyone was back living in them. I was introduced to the construction company that was responsible for lifting over 150 homes. I then spent the following five years moving over 150 homes into storage while they were being lifted, and then returned once they were completed.

From this I have become an absolute expert in the restoration business; an expert both self-proclaimed and third-party claimed. Relocators specializes in handling packouts for over fifty restoration companies, adjusters both public and independent, and even some high-end insurance carriers.

My experience prior to Sandy coupled with my knowledge and experience during and after Sandy puts me in a unique position to understand the business from many different angles.

Moving is one of life's most stressful things, but moving after fire or water damage compounds the stress. Years later, Florida was hit with a catastrophic hurricane. Relocators has a very big clientele in Florida because we have been moving people there for years. I wound up partnering with a charitable organization called angelsoflongisland.com and sending two full trucks of supplies down to the victims of the hurricane. We wound up staying and opening up in Florida on a local level. Through one of our New York restoration contacts, our first work was helping people on an island called Sanibel Island. Sanibel Island is a really gorgeous, upscale island near Fort Myers. It's supposed to be a place in America that few people know about. It's mostly populated by older, very wealthy people. I was at a town hall Zoom meeting with about fifty elderly people who were running the island. Our job was to give them advice as well as a plan of action on what was going to happen with all the damage and salvageable contents. At the end of the meeting, we opened up for questions. One woman said, "I understand you said that everything inside the house is your insurance company's responsibility. Also, that the items outside the house are not going to be covered by homeowners insurance, except your car, because for your car you just have to call your car insurance company. But what if the car in the garage port isn't your car?" In the sweetest elderly voice this poor woman continued, "the darn thing must have floated in." I thought to myself, *Oh boy; these people are in trouble!*

THE BONUS STORY

LUCK BE A LADY

During an estimate for a potential online auction I met the sweetest 88-year-old widow and discovered that she had active cancer and heart failure and was also on dialysis. As I looked at the items in her home, I got lost in the emotion of the life she must have had and her current condition. You could tell this lady had really lived! She had high-end purses and watches, jewelry, perfume, the latest technology, brand new Apple products, and much more. I am not implying that things are what make you live a full life. However, being there the things helped tell that story about her, basically she was into everything and you could imagine the affairs she had been to.

We sat down at the table with her live-in nurse and she began to tell me her situation. Her landlord told her she had 60 days to leave the house—nonnegotiable. The homeowner was beside herself. I assured her we would take care of everything for her within 55 days. Knowing I had to move our schedule around to make this work, I made it a priority, as no 88-year-old, let alone one with health conditions, should be faced with these issues.

Photo day came and, as we took pictures for her auction, all she talked about was how she had once lived a high-profile lifestyle with her husband, who was in a popular jazz band. He'd played at the UN and prestigious social clubs in New York City. Whenever she spoke about her past, she would smile. So I kept asking her stories about various items in the house. As scary as her transition was, she was excited to see what the future had in store. I was happy that the earlier vision I had for her life seemed to align with her memories.

The auction ended, and pickup day came fast. Normally we have rules that say the homeowner cannot be in the home during the sale process when their items are being picked up. We do this to protect both the buyers and the seller. The process is just too emotional and we try to avoid conflicts. In this case the rules had to be broken because of her mobility. We made sure she was comfortable and not overwhelmed for the emotional 6 hours she was about to endure.

She was very quiet during the pickup, not her usual chatty self. I gave her space to let her process everything. I was starting to worry. Either she was going to get angry at us or sad for herself; neither I wanted for her. When I went upstairs, I found her standing alone, staring out the window. She was so fixated on everything that was going on. My nerves were peaking. I was hesitant to ask if she was okay because she seemed to be in such a deep state. I waited and tried, and waited some more. Finally about 15 minutes later I let it go, I asked, "Everything okay? Do you need anything?" She turned around with a big smile and said, "This is such a fantastic way to meet men." I was flabbergasted. "I want to go outside," she said. I said, "Okay, let's go." She grabbed my arm and we slowly walked down the steps. "So you're looking for a man?" I said. She replied, "Of course I am. Why do you think I'm moving my king-size bed? I'm old, not dead."

As promised, within 55 days, we completed the auction and moved her into her new senior living community, where hopefully, all of her wildest dreams came to fruition!

THE ADVICE

Helping an elderly parent move can be challenging for all involved. For the elderly person, the move can be emotional, especially if they're moving due to illness or the death of a spouse. Having to then live alone, share living space with family members, or relocate to an assisted living or elder care facility adds additional levels of emotional complexity. Not only that, but the loss of freedom and any grief the senior might be experiencing can compound the stress of the physical and logistical aspects of moving. These same circumstances may present their own set of challenges for the person helping them move, which is often an adult child or family member. For those reasons and more, keeping the lines of communication open and allowing the senior to make their own decisions are important first steps. It's also important to focus on the change as a new beginning, rather than as an end.

Allowing seniors to express their feelings and concerns about the move will help them to feel heard, understood, and respected. Communicating that you are there to listen and help can go a long way toward setting their mind at ease. Actively listening to them throughout the process, being transparent and nonjudgmental, and including them in the decision-making can infuse positivity into the situation and help to alleviate any emotional burdens they may be carrying.

Many seniors may not want to move. A study by AARP showed that more than 75% of people over 50 prefer to remain in their communities as they age. It can be helpful to first consider the senior's preferences and the reasons they should or should not move. Safety features such as shower poles, and stair lifts, among others; can help a senior to remain in their home.

As parents age, it can be beneficial to talk about any safety concerns you have for them before they become an issue. Finding out earlier on what will help them to feel safer in their current environment and asking what they need can prevent problems down the road. Would they benefit from a security system or voice-activated communication equipment and smart home devices?

One of the most important first steps before the move is to come up with an action plan. What does the senior need to have in their new home, and what is provided and what is not? Putting the plan down on paper and making checklists can help facilitate the process, add transparency, and help make sure nothing is missed. It also helps that they have something to refer to on their own. We all know seniors tend to be forgetful.

Ensure that their new location is accessible in the ways they need it to be. Making sure things like wheelchair ramps and accessible entryways and tubs or showers are important. If they're moving into a facility, it's a good idea to find out what amenities and services are provided.

Begin the purging and packing process as early as possible. As you sort through the senior's items, give them the chance to talk about any memories. This can allow them to process their emotions around what is a major life transition. Infusing a sense of fun into the process can help lighten things up. Take breaks to watch favorite films, listen to the music of their choice, make snacks, or do anything else that makes them happy and reminisce.

As with the packing process, it's a good idea to allow more time for unpacking than you normally would for a different type of move. Divide the task of unpacking into small, easily manageable steps, taking it one room at a time. Set up items like photos, decorations, and memorabilia that help the senior to feel at home. Setting up their space as it was in their previous location can add a sense of familiarity to new surroundings. Do what you can to make them feel as comfortable as possible and listen to their concerns along the way. Always make sure to have their favorite recliner, or chair they like to sit on loaded last into the truck and first out of the truck.

"Senior move managers" specialize in helping seniors move. They facilitate everything from purging, sorting, and organizing to hiring movers, arranging donations and estate sales, and unpacking. You can find out more by contacting the National Association of Senior & Specialty Move Managers. Caring transition specialists offer similar services as senior move managers and hold a Certified Relocation Transition Specialist (CRTS) certification.

Look into any activities that may be of interest for the elderly person prior to the move. This can give them something to look forward to and help them to feel more settled in their new location. Check out any community events or classes available in their area, and any events calendars if they are moving into an assisted living facility or senior care home. Look over the events with them and ask if they see anything that interests them, then help them sign up if needed.

Emphasize the positives, like connecting with new people and getting involved in their community. A fresh start can be a great opportunity to provide new perspective and infuse a sense of excitement into an emotionally challenging process. Visiting a senior as often as possible can help them to feel better about the change. Encourage children and other family members to visit them in their new home often. This also gives you an opportunity to talk through any concerns they may have and to make sure they have everything they need.

> **Extra, extra!** *I cannot stress enough that if you're moving mom or dad out of your childhood home, make sure you take video or pictures of every space as it is prior to anyone rearranging or packing anything. One day, someone might pay a small fortune to have those kinds of memories. It's simple and can be fun to do it alongside mom or dad.*

THE REAL-WORLD HACKS

1. **Arrival thought.** If moving into an assisted living facility, always immediately engage the senior in whatever is happening at the moment with the rest of the community. Spare them the congestion of the actual move taking place.

2. **Plan for the new space.** When considering what to donate, store, or sell, consider how much living space the senior will have. Taking measurements of the available space in their new location and measuring any furniture will give you an idea of what they can take with them.

3. **Yes or no?** With the senior's buy-in, sort things into "yes" and "no" piles during the purging process.

4. **Access to services.** Look into any services (like pharmacies, grocery stores, and medical facilities) the seniors will need in their new area and ensure they have easy access to them.

5. **Address changes.** Don't forget to change the address with insurance and medical providers, financial institutions, pharmacies, and any other services, and to submit a change of address form with the USPS.

6. **Insure the future.** For long-distance moves, you may need to switch insurance providers, financial institutions, and pharmacies. Doing this in advance of the move will make the transition easier for the senior and ensure they have access to the services they need in their new location.

7. **Consider accessibility.** Does their new location have everything they need, like wheelchair ramps, stairlifts, and walk-in tubs, or do these things need to be installed?

8. **Safe transport.** When arranging medical transport services, consider what the provider offers vs. what the person they're transporting

will need. Are they equipped to handle any medical equipment the senior depends on, like oxygen tanks? Do they offer door-to-door assistance to help the senior from vehicle to home?

9. **Allow for emotional processing.** Remember that moving, especially under certain circumstances, can be emotional for an elderly person. Allowing them time to share their memories, grieve, and process emotions can help them to work through the process and prepare for what is—especially at their age—a major life change.

10. **Take it easy.** Take frequent breaks during the packing process and break everything into small, manageable tasks. This could include packing one room or closet at a time.

11. **Focus on the positives.** Discussing any benefits of the move can help give the senior something to look forward to. This can include services that are provided in the new location that will help make things easier for them, better access to medical care, a safer environment, being closer to friends and family, and less to clean or manage.

12. **Enlist help.** Involve the seniors in the process and allow them to make decisions. It's important for them to retain a sense of autonomy.

13. **Infuse a sense of fun.** Play music of their choice during the move and take breaks to look through photo albums, watch favorite films, or reminisce about the past. These memories will be invaluable to you as well as them.

14. **Team effort.** Enlist the help and support of friends and family, and keep everyone in the loop. Communicate your needs and those of the senior to everyone who needs to know. Let them know your plans and provide them with the senior's new contact information.

15. **Comfort matters.** Keep your loved one comfortable, especially if they suffer from dementia or illness.

16. **Let them be involved.** Suggest tasks your loved one can do, such as making phone calls and labeling boxes.

17. **Everyone in the loop.** Communicate plans with family members and keep everyone important to the senior in the loop through the transition.

18. **Keep in touch.** Exchange contact information with any friends they are leaving behind.

THE CONCLUSION

When I was a kid, my mother started an estate sale company because her mother was sick and needed to move into our family home. Years later I would clean out the houses after my mother's sales. It is here where I met directors of assisted living facilities, one being Steven Pike, who is featured below. Steven did not like the movers constantly coming to his facility, and pretty much twisted my arm into renting trucks and moving clients into his facility. It made sense because the clients already knew me because they were mutual clients of my mother. I offered a more intimate approach and had a connection to the senior. This is how I initially got into my career. One thing that I always observed with senior moving is that they are very combative and contentious with the family they love who are trying to help them. I think you can draw parallels to a child being angry that they are reprimanded by a parent when the parent is just trying to protect them. Again as other times, here the cycle of life comes full circle.

However, I will tell you one thing: I was always treated extra special by the elderly client I was moving. I remember at times as a young adult often being mistaken for the grandson and not the mover.

MOVING THE ELDERLY

I say this because it is so easy to lose patience with an elderly person. Especially while processing through a long drawn-out difficult situation like moving. The stranger however, is a fresh ear and ally to the elderly person. They get excited about telling their stories to the mover who, unlike the family, hasn't heard them a million times. If you throw away everything from this chapter you can greatly help your senior transition by just following these two tips.

First, have patience with the senior and try to value their input and stories even if you have heard them so much you could recite them. Secondly, ask the company you hire to send personnel who are experienced with moving seniors. If you could afford it, maybe even send an extra worker; one they can dedicate to holding the senior's hand during the actual move. A great first impression of the mover will really help with the emotion throughout the day.

> **BONUS TIP:** If Medicare becomes an issue, there are brokers like Ken Gewanter of *keng@stressfreebenefits.com* who assist at no cost to the senior. These brokers help find the best plans to cover as many medical expenses as possible.

THE EXPERTS

Andrew M. Lamkin, Esq., Estate Planning Attorney

When moving, it is vitally important to safeguard all of your important estate planning documents, such as wills, trusts, powers of attorney, and health care proxies. Additionally, relocation to a different state may necessitate meeting with an estate planning attorney in that new state to ensure that your existing estate plan continues to protect you and your family, as different state laws may require an update of your plan.

Steven Pike, Owner of Integrity Home Care NY

My name is Steven Pike and I am the owner of Integrity Home Care NY. We provide home care services to help seniors stay in their home when they need assistance and it is no longer safe for them to be alone. Integrity Home Care NY has one main focus—to keep a loved one in their home safely. We work directly with families and clients to figure out a schedule, a plan of care, and the right caregiver for the job. Nothing we do is permanent and we are there as long as the family needs the support.

We are also there to support people when they make the decision that staying in their home is no longer a safe option. Moving someone out of their forever home is extremely difficult and anxiety-filled, with so many moving parts. Two of the pieces of moving that can be delegated out are the actual move and what to do with the furniture or possessions that cannot be moved to the downsized home or to a place like an assisted living facility.

I used to do marketing for assisted living facilities and helping families with finding a safe choice for a loved one. Once they made a decision on placement, most families never knew where to turn for help with the moves or the estate sales when moving mom or dad into the facility. Some got overcharged, some never got callbacks, and others felt pressured. It was part of my job to help these families with guidance on who could help with these next steps. I met Robert through his mother, Denise, who did estate sales and had come in to talk about her services. As a kid, for side money, Rob was helping his mother's clients clean out their homes after his mother's estate sales. Getting to know Rob and knowing the contention of moving clients into my facilities, I used to enlist Rob to rent box trucks and do the small moves. This way I knew the elderly clients were in good hands. We gave him a try as a resource to our clients. He never failed, and we got great reviews, so we put his name out to all of our other locations as a great asset, and he did not fail them either.

Some of the things that I have learned along the way are that constant communication is essential, and having the right network of friends, family, and co-workers to turn to, and having good people surrounding you at all times, are key. Our company lives by the word integrity and always doing the right thing; not everyone does this.

14

MOVING PETS

"I'm open for possibilities. I'm open for choices. I always welcome new ideas. I'm always eager to learn. I'm never going to close my mind from learning."

—Cesar Milan

Under every turn

I will never forget the feeling of waking up knowing that I had to cleanout a hoarder's house the upcoming day. If you have ever seen the show *Hoarders* or experienced being in a hoarder's house, you will know what I'm talking about. The ones that are really bad could make it hard for you to eat breakfast prior to even arriving; forget midday lunch break.

I remember early on we were cleaning out the home of someone who hoarded beer cans. Their house was like the ball pit in a children's play area; but instead of balls there were empty cans strewn all over. The entire main area of the house was filled with beer cans from the floor to the ceiling. This was not such a bad situation, and I remember being pleasantly surprised. This was nothing like the house we had cleaned out the week before, where one room was filled with used adult diapers and the home had no accessible facilities. There was a room with all the adult diapers in it—used adult diapers. This day was different and the smell of beer cans was a pleasant respite from the types of repulsion we were used to encountering. I definitely let down my guard and was working at a fast, yet relaxed, pace. As the living room started to clear, I along with an employee, went to lift up the old sofa. The client was to my right and I remember I could see her out of the corner of my eye. I lifted the couch and instantly dropped it and jumped back. The woman ran towards me and asked what happened. I said, "Ma'am, there is a perfect full body skeleton of a cat." The woman said, "Oh my god. We've been looking for her for years!"

THE ADVICE

Pets are especially sensitive to changes in routine and schedules, and a move is one of the most disruptive life events there is—for humans and animals. Animals are sensitive to changes and can become confused and frightened when their environment is disrupted.

During the move itself, designate an area to keep your pets in, like a quiet part of the house, while the movers are in and out of your home. Keeping cats and dogs in crates or carriers helps ensure they don't bolt when the door is opened. Check on your pet often to let them see you and to reassure them that you're there.

To help pets feel more secure, stick to their routine as much as possible during the transition process. That may mean taking Fido for walks at the same time you normally would and sticking to the feeding schedule. Your best option is probably to hire a pet sitter, or placing your pet in daycare is another option that can help your pet avoid the confusion, clamor, and stress of moving.

Before you bring your pet into your new home, pet-proof the home first. Place familiar objects like favorite toys and beds and lead them to these objects. Make sure the doors and windows are closed before you let them out of their crate or carrier so they don't become frightened and try to escape. Pets will sometimes return to their previous location, which is why exchanging contact information with your previous neighbors can come in handy.

Similar to dogs and cats, for fish, it's important to keep stress levels and disruption as low as possible. Stress, along with disruptions in their environment, can make fish more susceptible to illness. Keep in mind that it's better not to feed fish for 24 hours before you put them in their transport containers. The reduction in waste they produce keeps ammonia levels low in their transport environment. Fish can live for as long as a week without food, so don't worry!

Transporting fish in water from their tank reduces possible impacts to their health. You can carry them in plastic bags or bowls that have a zip cover. Bear in mind, though, that plastic bags will only retain enough oxygen for fish to survive for about an hour. (If you have to travel further with your fish, you can use a battery-powered air pump to keep oxygen flowing into their water.) Use a siphon to move the water from the fish tank to a clean plastic tub or bucket (or several) with a lid that fits over it securely.

Before moving fish to their travel containers, first turn off any filters, heaters, and pumps. If you use a heater, let it cool down for about half an hour before taking it out of the tank. This will allow the equipment to regulate the temperature and avoid compromising it. Siphon about 80% of the tank's water into lidded containers and then place water into the transport containers. Remove fish with a net and place them in their bags or bowls before removing plants, gravel, and decorations from the tank.

After doing this, remove plants first and then the decor, and siphon out the rest of the tank's water before removing the gravel or substrate. It's really ideal to remove the substrate before transporting the tank, because its weight can cause damage to the seals on the tank during transport. Don't rinse the gravel or substrate, though, because it contains bacteria native to the fish tank. Carefully wrap and pack all aquarium items and seal gravel in clean, waterproof containers, like bags or plastic containers. Your best bet is to transport fish direct to location in a personal vehicle.

Before setting up the aquarium in your new home, make sure you have all your fish tank supplies unpacked first. Re-add the substrate and decorations, then pour the aquarium water from the buckets or containers back into the tank. This is the 80% you siphoned out before the move. You can then add the heater, filter, and pumps and turn them on. Allow the heater to reach the temperature you need for your tank before reintroducing fish into the water. Fish should be introduced slowly back into their environment. First, allow their bags to float on the surface of the water for about three quarters of an hour before releasing them into the water and keep the lights off for several hours to minimize stress on the fish. Some tanks may require dechlorinated water to be added to the tank, so some preparation might be required for the water you add to fill the tank back to the appropriate water level.

Pets like gerbils, hamsters, birds, snakes, and guinea pigs can be transported in their cages or terrariums. Make sure they have sufficient water and food at all times during the move. Put cages in your personal vehicle and be sure your pet has plenty of oxygen; when traveling in vehicles packed full of belongings, items can easily shift and cover cages and terrariums.

Make sure cages and terrariums are stable and secure and that all doors and access points are latched so you don't wind up dealing with a surprise escape attempt. Imagine trying to find a hamster or a snake in an SUV filled with stuff! Buckle the cage or terrarium in the back of the vehicle to prevent it from toppling or sliding en route. If a cage falls over, doors can become unlatched, and terrarium covers could slide open. For reptiles that require an external heat source, you can purchase a battery-powered heat lamp.

THE REAL-WORLD HACKS

1. **All's well.** Stick to your pet's routine and schedule as much as possible to help them feel a stronger sense of normalcy.

2. **A safe space.** Have crates and carriers ready for moving day. Keep cats and dogs crated during the move so they don't become frightened and try to make a run for it.

3. **Familiar objects.** Especially for cats and dogs, a familiar object in their crate or carrier, like a blanket or toy with their scent on it, can help them to feel more secure.

4. **Be there for them.** Make your presence known. Checking on your pet regularly and letting them see you can bring them a sense of calm.

5. **Feeding schedule.** Make sure your pets stay hydrated and are fed at the usual times.

6. **Advance preparation.** Find and register with a veterinarian in your new location before moving.

7. **Prepare for the introduction.** Pet-proof your new home before you introduce cats and dogs to the unfamiliar environment.

8. **Retention plan.** Keep pets indoors—either in crates, carriers, or in a room with the door shut—while the movers are there to prevent them escaping.

9. **Necessities close at hand.** Pack a bag with your pet's necessary items and set it aside so it doesn't accidentally find its way onto the moving truck.

10. **Well equipped.** Familiarize yourself with the equipment (and process) you'll need to safely prepare fish for a move.—before you begin the process.

11. **Buckle in.** Buckle cages and terrariums into the backseat of your personal vehicle to prevent them from sliding or toppling during transit.

12. **Batten down the hatches.** Make sure all doors to small animal cages are securely latched and terrarium covers are secured.

THE CONCLUSION

The first night I ever had my dog he immediately went to the bathroom on our living room throw rug. The next day I saw that my wife had put the rug in the garbage. I removed it from the garbage and put it all the way in the very back of the yard where I wanted to train the dog to go to the bathroom. The trick actually worked well and my dog has been going in the spot where I put the rug ever since. Animals are creatures of habit and instinct. When transitioning with a pet be sure to use this as an opportunity to possibly correct some behaviors you had previously not had the chance to.

> **BONUS TIP:** If you're moving long-distance or internationally, you might consider hiring a pet transport company. As you would before hiring any company though, be sure to check that they are licensed and read their customer reviews before making your decision.

THE EXPERT

Andy Hanellin

My name is. Andy Hanellin I have been training dogs for over 40 years. I have trained thousands of dogs for a multitude of jobs: for the police, service dogs, therapy dogs, and best friend and have moved at least 10 times over the years. Moving is stressful enough on us as humans, and all that stress is passed on to our dogs, so here are a few tips to make that transition easy:

1. *Update Identification and Microchip Information:* Before moving, make sure your pets' identification tags and microchip information are up-to-date with your new address and contact details. This will help ensure their safe return if they were to get lost during the move or in the new neighborhood.

2. *Pack a Pet Essentials Bag:* Put together a bag specifically for your pets with their essentials. Include items such as food, water, bowls, medications, toys, blankets, and any other items they may need during the moving process and the first few days in the new home. Having these items easily accessible will help keep your pets comfortable and reduce stress.

3. *Keep Your Pets in a Safe and Secure Area:* On moving day, it's best to keep your pets in a quiet and secure area of the house, away from all the hustle and bustle. This will prevent them from getting anxious or accidentally escaping during the moving process. Consider using a crate or a designated room with their familiar belongings to help them feel secure.

4. *Arrange Pet-Friendly Accommodations:* If you're moving long-distance and need to stay overnight at hotels or other accommodations, make sure to book pet-friendly places in advance. Check their pet policies, any additional fees, and ensure they have appropriate facilities for your pets.

5. *Stick to Your Routine:* Pets thrive on routine, and moving can disrupt their sense of familiarity. Try to maintain their regular feeding, exercise, and playtime

schedule as much as possible. This will provide them with a sense of stability and help reduce stress.

6. Gradually Introduce Your Pets to the New Home: When you arrive at your new home, introduce your pets to one room at a time. Start with a quiet and comfortable area where they can acclimatize gradually. Gradually expand their access to other areas of the house as they become more familiar with the new environment.

7. Give Your Pets Time to Adjust: Moving can be stressful for pets, and it may take some time for them to adjust to their new surroundings. Be patient and give them the time and space they need to settle in. Provide them with plenty of love, attention, and reassurance during this transition period.

8. Maintain a Sense of Humor: This is going to be stressful enough on you and whatever you feel you'll pass on to your pets, so laugh at the things that are funny. Keep a lighthearted attitude when dealing with your animals. The last thing you want is to come home and find that your pet was nervous and peed on your brand new $5000 couch.

Remember, every pet is unique, so it's important to consider their individual needs and make adjustments accordingly. By taking these suggestions into account, you can help make the moving process smoother and less stressful for both you and your pets.

Sweat in the Dojo relax in the battle field

15
DIY MOVES

"I long, as does every human being, to be at home wherever I find myself."

–Maya Angelou.

4:20 Transport

We were moving a client from Los Angeles to New York and they needed help shipping their vehicles. They found someone on the internet and after speaking made what seemed to be the most economical and dependable choice. Their vehicle was shipped on an open double-decker with about maybe six to ten cars on the truck.

The day of the move I remember the client looking frustrated and angry. When I asked what was wrong, he told me that his car would not be arriving, indefinitely. He explained that a car on the bottom of the truck, closest to the cab, had caught on fire. What happened was the tire became flat and the rim sparked against the metal of the transporter probably when the truck hit a bump on the highway. The car on the bottom that caught on fire ignited in flames, which, in turn, started melting the car above it. When the car above it started melting from the flames, hundreds of pounds of marijuana started to fall out of the tires. It turned out that an illegal company was loading car tires with marijuana and transporting them, unbeknownst to the trucking company, across the country. My client's car did not get damaged because it was on the bottom tail end of the truck and the fire was caught in time, their car wasn't damaged. However, that did not really make the matter any better. My client was told he would have to wait months to receive his car because now it was held up by the DEA and there was nothing they could do about it. The fire happened somewhere in the Midwest, in the middle of nowhere. When the truck caught fire, it pulled into a gas station and essentially the whole town came out to see what was happening. It was all over the news because of the overwhelming smell of marijuana burning that filled the air. I remember thinking how much I would have loved to see the look on that truck driver's face when he realized what he was transporting.

THE ADVICE

How Much Does It Cost?

When it comes to hiring a moving company for a local or long distance move the price can vary greatly. In its simplest form, the cost is based on men per hour and materials. The main factors that affect the cost are in

DIY MOVES

relation to the distances of each location from each other, the type and amount of contents, and the logistics of each location. Typically things like, stairs, elevators, long walks, distance from the first location to the second location, distance from either location to the company's base, how fragile the items are, is packing of small items needed, are places for the items planned out, are all factors that will help to determine the cost of a move.

Local moves are typically charged based on men per hour. Whereas long distance moves are typically based on weight or cubes. Cubes are slang for the cubic feet of the contents. To give you an example, a typical 26-foot moving van with a gross vehicle weight of 26,000 lbs can be driven by anyone with a regular class D license. The weight is important because they make these trucks as big as possible before they are mandated to need a CDL license to drive them. A truck this size usually accommodates a 3 to 5 bedroom home and holds about 1800 cubes.

So to understand what this all means we must understand that cubic feet is measured by calculating length x width x height of an object. If you measured every single item in your home and then added each item up you would get the cubic feet of the contents of your home. This number you can use to determine what truck size you need to move your home. This is how moving companies estimate the truck and manpower they will need for your move. Another trick here would be to use 50 cubes per man per hour as a rule of thumb.

An example would be this: let's say I determine that I have 1800 cubes of contents in my home. I multiply that number by two, (the load, and the unload) I get 3600 total cubes to be moved. I then divide that number by 50 and my result is 72 man hours of work to complete my move. Remember to note that this number does not include the time to get from the first location to the final location. This is just labor time. So if I take the 72 man hours and divide it by the number of hours I want my move to take; let's say 10 hrs. Then I will know I need 7.2

men or about 7 men for 10 hours plus transport in between locations in order to complete my move.

At any time you can do a quick Google search to see what the average moving costs are in your area. I do not recommend this data and typically find that the numbers are skewed. Factors like the low labor rates in rural areas tend to skew the data. You can also call in inventory or input inventory into web portals in order to get estimated costs for your move. Again, I do not recommend these options, either. The shortcuts with gathering estimates usually serve to be more of a hindrance than help. Your best bet always is to get three different on site or virtual estimates by a recommended and reputable moving company in your area.

For those that are inclined to handle their move themselves these estimating tips above can still help to ensure you can gauge what you will need come moving day. If you originally planned on hiring a moving company and then decided against it, you can still use the estimated men and materials as a baseline for what you will need.

If you're planning to move yourself, you'll need to figure out the right truck size. Truck rental companies list the size of trucks in feet, along with their capacity in cubic feet. To find out the best truck size—so you're not shorted and left with items you have no place for, and so you don't wind up with a bigger truck than you need, with items sliding around in the empty space—measure everything you're moving after it's packed. To find the cubic feet, multiply the length by the width by the height (LxWxH). It's easiest to make a list of everything you're moving first and write down the measurements. Once you have those down, add them up, and this will give you the approximate cubic feet.

A 26-foot moving truck contains roughly 1,800 cubic feet; a 24-foot truck has about 1,600 cubic feet. You can easily do a Google search to find out what each size is in comparison to its rough cubic feet or check the truck rental company's website. A typical 3-bedroom home will fill a 24-foot or 26-foot moving truck. When in doubt, choose the next size up. You'll also want to make sure the truck will physically fit in both locations. If you have multiple stops to make to pick up items, consider renting a truck with side doors to make it easier to load and unload items. If you have large or heavy items, like pianos and pool tables, a truck with a lift gate will allow you to roll the dolly with the furniture up the ramp and into the truck, and vice versa.

If you're driving a box truck for the first time, make sure you're aware of the road rules. This includes knowing what bridges you can go under and what parkways you can drive on. You could create a catastrophe by traveling on a parkway and hitting a low bridge.

Enlisting your friends to help in exchange for pizza and beer is the timeless concept that comes to mind when we think of moving ourselves. I am all for saving money on a move but I think paying for good labor is important even on DIY moves.

If you're using hired labor, check the reviews before choosing someone. Make sure the reviews are mainly positive and current. There are many websites that offer moving labor helpers that are independent contractors. Some of these workers are very experienced and have a good self-employed, for hire operation. Just know that the communications and backing you would receive from hiring a company will not be comparable.

As a seasoned mover, I always choose newsprint paper over bubble wrap. Newsprint or packing paper is basically newspaper without the print on it. We have moved some of the highest-end houses and we don't use bubble wrap. Crumpled newspaper provides good cushioning for fragile items. You can also use what you already have to wrap breakables, such as dish towels, hand towels, washcloths, curtains, and linens. For packing materials, home improvement stores are usually the least expensive.

A few other things to consider: Where are you getting your blankets? How are you protecting your belongings? Blankets can be expensive. You might need 100 blankets for a three-bedroom house, which might cost about $2,000. Renting blankets will probably be your best option so you do not have to purchase blankets for only one move. To save money, use your least important blankets and towels and wrap all the blankets in stretch wrap.

What are you putting on the moving truck and what are you putting in your personal vehicle? It's better to put TVs in a pickup truck bed or in the backseat of a car, if possible. Anything fragile should be transported in your personal vehicle. Ideally, only professional movers should load fragile items onto a moving truck.

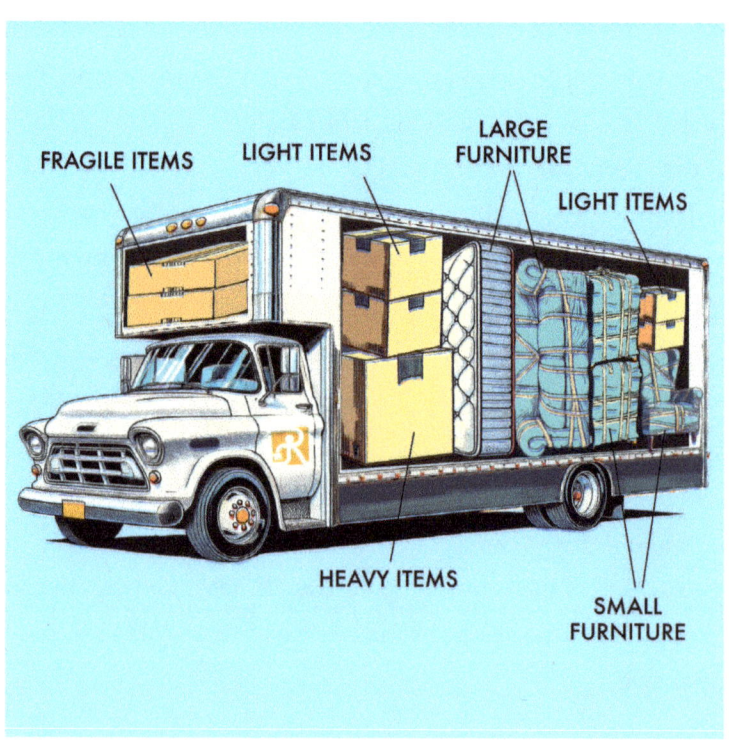

There are best practices when it comes to loading a truck or a moving pod. The way you load is extremely important so that you're protecting your belongings and maximizing the available space. Everything should be loaded in tiers, as described below.

Start with the heavy bases, which could be a long bureau or a long dresser, in the back of the truck or storage container. These should be completely wrapped in a blanket with tape or stretch wrap around them. Next to the heavy bases, you could stand a couch upright so it fills in the tier. On top of the dresser, you could put chairs interlocking with each other, all blanket-wrapped. Wardrobe boxes are a great place to put chairs, especially if you really want to protect them. You can stack boxes on top of the dresser. Above the couch, you could stuff soft goods, like garbage bags filled with blankets or pillows. Once you have a full tier, which means that nothing else can fit in that tier, you then grab a base to start the next tier and that's how a truck or storage container—anything that's going to be moved—needs to be packed.

If you leave 6 inches to a foot open on top of the tiers, you have a flat surface area where you can put packed flatscreen TVs, packed glass, packed picture frames—things that have cardboard or blankets around them but that are long and thin. Place oddly shaped items, like barbecue grills and coolers, last on the truck.

Make sure to wrap soft goods with blankets and stretch wrap, not just stretch wrap. If you turn a couch on its side so it's standing vertically, make sure there are blankets around the edges of the couch and then stretch-wrap the couch so it's protected. If you place it vertically on the floor of the truck, make sure you put another pad or cardboard down at the bottom of the truck for more protection. The last thing you want is the couch shimmying in the truck little by little and creating major scrapes or dirt marks in your truck. Stretch wrap alone is not sufficient for protection.

After you have loaded a few tiers, you should use straps to secure your belongings in the truck. There are E tracks on the left and right sides of trucks, where you can clip the straps on both sides, pull the strap through, and then wind it to tighten it.

For junk removal, if you're going to rent a dumpster, make sure you understand that renting a dumpster and hiring the labor may account for 70% to 80% of the cost of hiring a junk removal company. A dumpster could cost $800 and to make a few trips to the dump for a junk removal company with a dump truck, it could cost about $150 to $200 per load. Moving helpers will add to the costs. In the end, you may have spent 70% or more of what it would have cost to hire a junk removal company and you may have done a lot of work that you didn't need to do.

Offering things for donation or for free is a great way to purge things. I always say sell first, then offer your items for free, then pay to throw them away—in that order. Donation places are usually a waste of time. Don't depend on two people to come from a secondhand store and take your old couch. They're going to show up and cherry pick. They typically won't take anything heavy or difficult. They may take a few items and leave you with everything else.

Masonite is a great tool to protect your floors, especially if you have nice wood floors or flooring you want to keep from getting scratched or damaged. It's good to use, especially if your friends, who aren't professional movers, are helping you move.

One area that is especially prone to major damage is the top and bottom of staircases. Typically, when people are carrying something up or down the stairs, they drop it as soon as they reach the top or bottom to take a break. It's a good idea to tape a piece of Masonite in those locations or put down blankets or moving pads, but if you do so, be careful not to slip or get tripped up on a moving blanket, as you could fall down the stairs.

Unless it's previously negotiated, don't leave anything in your old location for the new homeowners. Especially if you're moving yourself, you may get tired and not want to move anything else. But unless it's pre-established and in writing from the real estate lawyers, if you leave anything that doesn't belong with the house, all you're doing is opening yourself up for a problem at the closing or the walk-through.

The house needs to be completely empty of everything that's not needed for the house, and this also applies to cleanouts. If you took your property, lifted it up, and turned it upside down, whatever falls out that's not organic, like firewood in the backyard, needs to be removed—unless, of course, it's something that goes with the house, like window air conditioners, the pole to open skylights, the garage door remote control, and possibly garbage pails. All appliances should stay, unless the contract indicates otherwise.

THE REAL-WORLD HACKS

1. **Clear it out.** Clear clutter before you pack. Donate or sell unwanted items to reduce the time you spend packing and to save time loading and unloading your belongings. Consider the 90/90 rule: If you haven't used something for 90 days and you don't think you'll use it in the next 90 days, it can go.

2. **Take the essentials.** Designate a box for items like toiletries, important paperwork, your wallet, and any clothing you'll need for before the move to the time you unpack. Clearly label it and set it aside so you can easily find it. If you're traveling by air or driving a personal vehicle to your new location, these items should be packed in a bag that's ready to take with you.

3. **Pack smart.** Crumpled newsprint paper provides excellent cushioning and is far less expensive than bubble wrap. Use a minimum one sheet per item.

4. **The tiered approach.** Pack the moving truck in tiers (see tips earlier in this chapter) and make good use of all available space, including drawers and the spaces under tables. Heavy items should go on the bottom, with lighter items stacked on top. Secure the load with straps every few tiers.

5. **Give it an inch, or several.** Leave about 6 inches to a foot of space at the top of tiers to place flat items, like packed TVs, packed pictures, and packed mirrors.

6. **Odds and ends.** At the end of the truck is where you put all the odds and ends, like patio furniture, grills, and anything that doesn't quite fit with everything else, like oddly shaped items.

7. **Last on, first off.** Remember, the last thing on the truck is the first thing off the truck.

8. **Cool it.** Be sure to have coolers ready to pack perishable food for short trips, especially if you're going to put it on the truck.

9. **Put it in grandma's attic.** Larger moving trucks have what's usually referred to as grandma's attic, and this is a great place to store fragile items. However, it's better to take fragile items with you in your personal vehicle, whenever possible, unless you're working with professional movers who are loading the truck or storage container.

10. **DIY?** If you're moving into a building, make sure you can move yourself. Some buildings require that you hire a licensed professional mover and keep their certificate of insurance on file.

11. **Be careful what you leave behind.** Don't leave anything behind in the house that doesn't belong with the house, like skylight poles or garage door remotes, unless it's specified in the contract that it should be left in the home.

12. **Check it off.** Especially if you're putting things into storage, make a checklist of what you need to bring with you before you start packing. That way, you don't mistakenly store items you will need.

13. **Ship it.** If you don't want to drive a truck, especially for longer moves, you can rent a shipping container and have it delivered to your new location.

14. **When to leave it to the pros.** Consider hiring professionals to move valuable and heavy items, like antique furniture, pianos, hot tubs, and appliances.

15. **Plan ahead.** Reserve your rental truck prior to moving and find out what the earliest start time is the day of the move. Ask if you could pick the truck up the night before for no additional charge.

16. **Does it measure up?** Always choose a bigger truck size than needed.

17. **Roll it in.** If you have large or heavy items, like pianos and pool tables, a truck with a lift gate will make loading easier. You can roll the dolly up the ramp and into the truck. However, these items are better left to professionals to move.

THE CONCLUSION

Usually when it comes to people moving themselves I often hear words like "never again." Often people do it once, or do it when they have to, and that experience encourages them to hire a company the next time around. Moving can be arduous and by the time you pay for the labor, equipment, materials, truck, fuel, the costs can be high. Doing all of this yourself will of course save you money, but it is important to also keep in mind the cost of time and take that into account as well. Coordinating all of this and then going and picking all of it up takes a lot of time all of which happens before and after any actual moving is done.

Personal time separate from any actual moving, damages, vehicle responsibility and cost of everything you need, are all items to take into consideration when deciding whether to hire a company or move yourself, renting a dumpster and hiring labor, or calling in a company. Decide if you're going to self-storage, filling out paperwork, and moving your items into a storage unit, or making a phone call to your mover to request your items be delivered back to your home. Deciding to hire a company or do it yourself will affect you economically, mentally, emotionally, and physically; it is up to you to decide what works best for you.

BONUS TIP: Three milliliter heavy duty contractor bags can be very helpful when moving yourself. Wrap towels, pillows and other soft goods in them.

DIY Moving | Hiring Movers

16 MOVING AUXILIARIES AND ODDITIES

"Your time is limited, so don't waste it living someone else's life. Don't be trapped by dogma, which is living with the results of other people's thinking. Don't let the noise of others' opinions drown out your own inner voice. And most important, have the courage to follow your heart and intuition. They somehow already know what you truly want to become. Everything else is secondary."

—Steve Jobs

LITTLE BROTHER, BIG PROBLEM

It was our first trip out of state and we could not have been more lost. The client was the sister of my dad's Captain at his firehouse. I had just started out and was excited about the opportunity to move her to Florida. This was going to be some adventure. We loaded up her furniture into a 24-foot rental truck. Of course, we did not know what cubes were, or how to estimate an out-of-state trip. We didn't even know how to get to Florida for that matter: it's basically one interstate highway the entire time.

We wound up having to load her outdoor items and some additional items into the back of our dump truck. The rental truck was full and we still had more stuff and I refused to let this woman down. We drove for about a day and a half only stopping for short naps on the side of the road. It was five of us split between the rental truck and the dump truck. We did not have a budget for hotels so upon arrival we planned to stop at my aunt's house in Stuart, Florida and crash there, then get up early the next day and unload the move. For two days there had been no rain but as we pulled into her complex the Florida skies opened up and torrential downpours started. We screamed for her to open the garage as we frantically unloaded the dump truck items into the garage. The next day it was sunny and we loaded the items back up and delivered them all to our happy client. All's well that ends well, sort of!

MOVING AUXILIARIES AND ODDITIES

After we unloaded we drove the rental truck to a drop-off location in a seedy part of town, hours from where we unloaded the truck. We all hopped in the dump truck and drove a couple hours to Tampa to stay at my cousin's house. When we got there everyone was thrilled to see us and it became an impromptu get together with cousins, aunts, and uncles. As we sat, relieved and enjoying ourselves amongst all the family and friends, I suddenly had an ""OH SHIT moment. I had left my work book in the rental truck which had my work binder containing cash and checks from three jobs totalling around $10,000. That was a million dollars to me at the time.

My little brother jumped into my cousin's Mustang and I jumped into the passenger seat and we sped out of his driveway the two hours back to the truck rental location. As we turned the first block we instantly got pulled over by the police. The officer was a short, southern young male, with an obvious disdain for people with a Yankee accent. I was clearly the mature older brother with responsibilities who was in a dire situation. As I explained my predicament he was understanding yet aggressive towards my brother. He was determined to find his marijuana; he stated multiple times how he caught a whiff and has a nose like a bloodhound. My brother adamantly denied having anything on him. I told the officer to just please allow us to keep going if I was successful in getting him to hand over whatever he had. The officer was equal parts angry at my brother and empathetic towards my situation. Finally, we were both outside the car watching him search the vehicle. Every second was like an hour for me; ironically, the officer finding something was the least of my concerns. Outside the car we were directed to throw an unknown pill that the officer had found in one of the cracks of the car which had nothing to do with us.

The officer then found a very small piece of joint in the ashtray. He belted out a loud "a-ha!" as he reveled in the success of "being right." I was instantly so relieved as he berated my brother. I was not concerned because I could clearly tell the officer was not going to do anything serious. I could just tell his fear-casting was a show of strength because he was going to just let us go. As I sat back in the car, all of a sudden I heard him yelling again. I looked up as I thought to myself, what now. Apparently my brother had been instructed to throw the small joint and instead he fake threw it and did some (want to be) magic trick by hiding the joint between his fingers. "You've got to be kidding me," I thought to myself. Now I started berating my brother as the officer took second fiddle to my frustration. This, in turn, seemed to please the officer and he gave my brother some final advice and let us get going.

As we got back to the car the officer repeatedly told my brother how lucky he was that he was sympathetic to my predicament and was letting us go.

As we drove away I rested my head against the window and buckled my seatbelt. My brother reached under the seat; in between his legs and pulled out his cigarette pack. He opened it and lit a full joint as he rolled down the window. I just looked in disbelief. "You're fucking joking, right?" He looked at me with a devil grin and said, "What, I saw him pull out. I clipped it and wedged it under my seat. There was no chance he was going to find it. Plus I left that roach in the ashtray as a diversion."

We spoke very little for the two-hour drive back to the truck lot. When the environment started to look tough, I knew we were close. Behind the rental building I saw a light on through a fence. The fence was locked but there was one attendant standing by a one-pump gas station the rental place had on site. The gate was locked. I thought to myself I should act very nonchalant. If I show urgency he may think I left something valuable and refuse me entry in order to check the trucks. I got his attention and waited for him to come by the fence. When he got close I said, "I returned my truck by this fence a few hours ago. Mind if I run and grab my folder real quick." He opened the gate and asked if I knew which truck. I did not, there were like 50 of the same

MOVING AUXILIARIES AND ODDITIES

exact trucks. He said, "over there are all the ones I am fueling up that came back tonight" as he pointed behind the fuel pump. I ran by them one by one and within a minute or two saw my big black binder on the dash and reached in and grabbed it. I zipped it open and saw everything I needed right in the flap. Ughh; what a weight off me. I yelled "thanks!" and jumped back in the car to finally end this never-ending trip.

THE ADVICE

Realistically, not all household items are shaped to facilitate neat, easily stackable loading. Some won't fit in a box—or a moving truck, for that matter. Bulky and unusually shaped things like swing sets, fish tanks, trampolines, tall floor lamps, and massive chandeliers may be a little trickier to move than most items.

And then there are the auxiliaries; think RVs and boats. RVs are notorious gas-guzzlers. Especially if you're embarking on a long-distance move, you may find it better to make a trip out of it and drive the RV to your destination. Read on for a few helpful pointers to help you navigate the relocation of life's more awkward items.

For fragile, valuable, and delicate items, like heirlooms and awards, packing them securely—if they're small enough to be packed—should be your first priority. Custom wood crates are essential for these types of items. Soft blankets or styrofoam around them with a hard wooden outer shell is the best technique.

Where they're placed on the moving truck (or in your personal vehicle) is also important. To ensure their safe transit, fragile and delicate items can be placed in the grandma's attic area of the moving truck—that is, the space in the box truck above the truck's cab. If you choose to transport them in your personal vehicle, be cautious of unwanted attention.

Mirrors, Wall Art, and TVs

Use soft blankets or padding to help protect mirrors and framed pieces against breakage. Tape padding around the frame and cut pieces of cardboard to tape around the front and back. You can also purchase foam corners for extra protection. Flat items like these should go on top of other items on the moving truck or in between soft items like mattresses. Standing them upright with other items beside them can result in damage unless the items are strapped securely within a tier with soft items.

If you've kept your original TV box, repack the TV in it and make sure it's protected, either with padding you add or the original styrofoam it came in. If you're using corrugated cardboard, purchase the thicker variety for added protection. You can also purchase padded boxes or double-wall or triple-wall corrugated cardboard.

Playground Equipment

For swing sets and playground equipment, having the original assembly manual on hand will be helpful when it comes to taking the equipment apart. Before you disassemble the equipment, take detailed pictures to use as a reference for when you put it back together. After removing the swings and packing them in a box or garbage bags, remove any ladders, slides, and monkey bars. Be sure to clearly label packed items and securely strap down the pieces in the truck. And, keeping all hardware together in a plastic bag and clearly labeling what it goes to can save you headaches later.

Note: Swing sets, along with some gym equipment, Murphy beds, and other items may have warranties that are voided if anyone except a licensed employee or agent disassembles or moves them. This is something you need to find out from the manufacturer or sales person who sold the item.

Musical Instruments

Pianos, organs, and harps are best handled by professional movers; there are also movers who specialize in piano moving. If your regular movers or moving helpers are loading a piano onto the truck, make sure the truck (if you've rented it yourself) has a ramp. If you're working with professional movers, let them know of any large or heavy objects they'll be moving when you get the estimate.

More portable instruments, like drums and guitars, should be wrapped with plenty of padding and are ideally transported in a personal vehicle. Disassemble things like drum kits as much as possible and pack items in boxes marked fragile. The black hard moving cases made custom for each instrument are always going to be the best practice when available. I am sure we all remember those big black items with handles we used to have to lug on and off the bus in elementary school.

Antiques and Heirlooms

It goes without saying that older items are often more fragile than newer ones and should be handled with extra care. For any items with drawers that need to be taped shut, make sure you are mindful about the finish. Wrap a loose blanket around the area with the drawers and then tape around the blanket. You can also flip the tape and attach it, by wrapping it around the item and leaving the sticky side facing out. Best practice when not crating an item would be to wrap it in padding, then a layer of cardboard, or masonite; then shrink wrap the item.

For especially valuable or fragile items, it may be best to hire professionals who specialize in transporting valuables and antique pieces. I have worked with companies that solely specialize in art and high-value item handling. These companies can be sought out in major cities. I have seen them move things like the Bill of Rights, Roman figurines, ceiling art from the 1700s, and major one-of-a-kind paintings to name a few.

Preparing Your Vehicle for Transport

For boats, RVs, and personal vehicles, driving them to your destination may not be an option. If you are considering driving your vehicle to the destination or having a friend do it for you, it's a good idea to weigh the costs of fuel against quotes from licensed motor carriers who will transport the vehicle.

RVs in particular cost a lot to refuel, and gas mileage may be about 6 to 10 mpg for class A motorhomes. For professional RV transport, there are generally three options available: you can hire someone to drive the vehicle to its destination, use flatbed shipping (which is sometimes a more affordable option if the carrier can transport your vehicle along with others), or you can drive it yourself.

Unless it's being driven, there are a few steps you'll need to take to prepare your RV for transport:

1. All items should be secured and all appliances turned off.
2. Remove anything hanging from the walls and ceiling, stow loose items, and secure latches and anything that slides out.
3. The power supply, along with water and gas lines, should be disconnected.
4. Your shipping company can supply recommendations on the ideal tire pressure for transit.
5. It's also recommended to make sure there are no leaks, the battery is in good condition, and fluid levels are within normal range.
6. Finally, make sure the tow bar and hitch are secured.

For boats, whether you're hauling them on a trailer or having them transported by a licensed carrier, there are a few things to do to prepare your watercraft for its journey by land:

1. First, make sure that the water and fuel levels are at no more than a quarter of the tank capacity.
2. All windows, doors, and hatches should be secured and the battery disconnected.

3. Stow anything that's loose in the boat to prevent it moving around during transit; this may include anchors, canvases, and cushions.

4. Before heading out, check the tires, latches, and lights on the trailer.

Before shipping personal vehicles:

1. Photograph the odometer and the vehicle's exterior and interior.

2. Secure or remove any loose items in the vehicle and check all fluid levels; make sure there are no leaks.

3. The battery should be fully charged and tires inflated to appropriate levels.

4. The fuel level should be at an eighth to a quarter of a tank.

5. Make sure to disable any alarms prior to transit.

6. Disabling or removing toll tags will prevent any unnecessary fees.

7. If someone is shipping your vehicle for you, it's ideal to have two sets of keys—one to provide to the carrier, and the other to keep on hand as backup. If you're down to one set of keys, it's better to have at least one copy made to give to the driver or shipper.

Grandfather clocks

I personally remember always thinking grandfather clocks were much more intimidating than they actually were. Your first bet is to open the front and remove the pendulum. It is basically on by a small hook and comes right off by gently lifting it up. Next step is to lift out each of the three hanging weights. These are the mini barrels that are hanging on chains next to the pendulum. Next step is to tape all of the chains against the inside of the clock so that they do not tangle in transport.

MOVING AUXILIARIES AND ODDITIES

Next close the front and lock it. Here STOP! The most common issue I have always encountered, believe it or not, is losing that tiny little antique key you use to lock the front. Place the key in a safe place and proceed. Next step is to wrap the entire clock in soft blankets and be sure to cover the bottom completely to avoid ugly scratches on the base. Tape the blankets around the clock. Then tape cardboard around the blankets in order to strengthen up the glass areas. Lastly, wrap the clock in shrink wrap and you are done.

THE REAL-WORLD HACKS

1. **Research before committing.** As mentioned elsewhere in this book, before hiring a professional, check their online reviews and how they respond to them (especially the negative ones), and look at their website. With art handlers it is important to know who their house accounts are. Looking for big name companies will guide you on who to hire.

2. **Filler items.** Fill empty spaces in hollow items like ceramic teapots with cushioning materials. Crumpled newspaper, washcloths, dishcloths, and hand towels make great filler.

3. **Sharp hack.** Cut cardboard to tape around items that don't fit in boxes, and use a razor knife to make cutting the cardboard easier.

4. **DIY art box.** After wrapping mirrors, framed pictures, and artwork in a blanket, tape pieces of cardboard to the front and back. You can add another layer of blankets or stretch wrap over this.

5. **Extra strength.** Use double- and triple-walled corrugated cardboard to protect glass and other breakable items.

6. **Crate it.** Consider using crates to transport valuable and large items, such as high-value art, heirlooms, antiques, and statuary. However, these items may be best left to professionals to prepare for transit.

7. **Cover your vases.** Cut cardboard to tape around large vases and similar breakable objects. Taping padding around these items before wrapping them in cardboard gives them an added layer of protection.

8. **DIY XL box.** Wardrobe boxes are great to use as on the spot, quick, crates. Irregular pieces can fit in them and you just have to wrap the item quickly in a soft blanket.

9. **Keep it together.** Take extensive pictures and videos of all items and hardware before disassembling anything.

10. **Separate the hardware.** Put hardware for disassembled items in plastic bags and label them with the name of the equipment or furniture they belong to. Put hardware in separate bags, so that one bag contains all of the hardware for a single piece of furniture or equipment.

11. **Don't void the warranty.** Before you move, check warranties to find out if a licensed professional is required to move the item. The warranty may be voided otherwise.

12. **Prevent an explosive situation.** If you're working with professional movers, let them know in advance if you need to move firearms, propane tanks, or anything toxic, corrosive, or flammable.

13. **A lengthy consideration.** Long items, like fishing poles, are at risk of breaking. When possible, disassemble them first. If they don't disassemble, tape around any connection points with masking tape. Wrap them in blankets or other padding and place them on top of the tiers in the truck or storage container.

14. **Document it.** Before shipping valuable items and vehicles, take detailed photos of the exterior and interior just prior to shipping,

MOVING AUXILIARIES AND ODDITIES

in case you need to file a claim for any damages later. Be sure to photograph the vehicle odometer reading as well.

THE CONCLUSION

I am sure there are auxiliary items I have not thought of or could even fathom. You do this long enough, you tend to see it all. In this chapter I tried to highlight all the most common, uncommon and difficult items you come across when moving. It is worth mentioning that taxidermy should always have custom crates. For those living in older city apartments these items below may also prove to be useful in a tough situation.

For old buildings with small elevators, the super can lower the elevator to floor level. Then a sofa can be put on the top of the elevator. Have the super manually call up the elevator to the desired floor and again lower it to floor level and remove the sofa. The movers will have to take the stairs or another elevator.

There are highly skilled companies that can cut any sofa, loveseat, or upholstered item in half and then reassemble it. I have seen this often and the expense is great. First, they charge a pretty penny and second, you have to coordinate it because they only cut and fix it. The movers have to take the items from the first to the second location in the same time frame the work is being done. So one service is being paid to wait on the other service at all times. But, where there's a will, there's a way.

> **BONUS TIP:** *Rigging* is when a heavy-duty trucking company uses a boom truck to hoist large pianos and other large items into penthouses in skyscrapers. For the more common problematic situations, the other tricks in the conclusion may work.

17
MOVING: AN EMOTIONAL JOURNEY

My mother always told me, "This too shall pass." This saying, which is thought to have its origins in Persian Sufi poetry, is a common one that spans cultures and history and one I have really come to rely on.

THE DAWN OF A NEW DAY

One of our estimators was working with a client who wouldn't or couldn't commit to a sale or a move. He had to be out but he was suffering from process paralysis. Initially, he spoke with our moving estimator before he was passed to me to discuss having a sale. When I spoke with the client, he said he was adamant about the fact that he was going to refuse talking on the phone with me, but he would change his mind because my name is Dawn—the name of the woman he loves.

My initial red flag meter was on high alert. Our goal is to help ease people's stress and I went ahead and booked this client anyway. Our original moving estimator felt that there was enough to do a sale. A challenging dynamic because essentially we booked a setup day, a tag sale, a move and a cleanout, with only the moving estimator actually walking the property.

First on the plan was the setup day for the sale. When it arrived, the employee who was first at the location called me and said, "You have got to come here now," so I did.

When I walked into the house, I could not believe what I was looking at. It was a complete hoarder situation. One large room was filled wall-to-wall and floor-to-ceiling with garbage—literally, actual garbage. I opened the door to the room and the smell was absolutely unbearable. I quickly closed the door and had to pretend, for this phase of the job, that the room didn't exist. As we went through items in the home, deciding what to sell, he kept saying, "No, I'll keep it. I don't want to part with it." Without argument, I let him go through his process. I am well-versed with the process and knew I had a special bond with him, considering my first name.

Prior to setting up the house for a sale, we needed to do a pre-clean-out in order to remove some of the junk. We took approximately 50 black garbage bags to the curb, which was about half of the minimum job we needed to do in order to set up. The movers were set to come 2 days later and the task of setting up for the tag sale couldn't be completed until the rest of the items were out of the location.

Upon leaving the house, the homeowner started going through the garbage bags. That's when the calls started coming in. He was yelling because we threw out garbage that was in his kitchen. I turned around and headed back to the house knowing face-to-face was my best line of defense. I let him vent and express his feelings, knowing that this was just part of the process for a hoarder. He found one old, beat-up sneaker in the garbage and absolutely lost his mind. He wanted that other sneaker, but of course it was not in the same garbage bag. Come hell or high water he had to find the part of the pair. So I dug down and started to help him look for it. I dug through all the garbage bags because I knew this would calm him down a bit; and it did. We couldn't find the other sneaker and his aggression and anger started morphing into sadness.

I looked him in the eye and calmly I said, "I know the sneaker holds meaning to you, like everything here, but at the end of the day, it's just a sneaker. All these items hold energy and the only way you can release that energy is to get rid of the items. The memory of the loved one will still remain." He said, "Yeah, right. I'll never escape this hell." After an awkward few moments I left him on the floor partially sobbing and surrounded by black bags. There was nothing more I could do at the moment.

Two days passed, and it was time for both the setup and move day to take place simultaneously. Knowing about the dynamic I arrived at the house early for the setup, about an hour into the moving process. I immediately was on alert when I saw items he said he wasn't selling, not packed in the truck. I told the movers, "Hey, you forgot these items." The mover said, "No, he decided to sell all that." I summoned the homeowner to make sure the job was correct and alert him about the mistake. But the client looked different. Nothing had changed but he radiated differently than he had before. He was beaming from ear to ear as he said, "Dawn, you were right. I'm sick and I'm a two-time cancer survivor. I have so much to be thankful for. After my marriage, I dated a woman who I loved dearly. She told me she was a widow. After 4 years of dating, one day, she turned to me and said, "You have to leave. My husband is getting out of jail and he will kill you." He continued to tell me how he was beyond heartbroken. Three months later, she committed suicide because she couldn't leave her husband and that's when he became severely depressed, to the point that it was debilitating. He'd recently met a woman named Dawn. She'd completely turned his life around and he was happy again for the first time in 12 years. He told me he had an epiphany after the first day of the setup because of what I said to him. He realized that all those items were just masking this depression he had been carrying. He now realized he was burying his feelings in stuff, to escape having to confront how he really felt. He said my line about how all of those items carry energy played in his head that entire night. The next day he woke up and felt he was ready to let that energy go and move on to the next chapter of his life.

THE ADVICE

Moving is hard. We naturally form attachments to the places we live and the people around us. Relocating due to a divorce or the death of a loved one can introduce an additional level of complications. Giving yourself time to process difficult emotions or to celebrate joyful ones can help pave the way for a fresh start.

Not only does relocating incur financial costs, it can also take an emotional toll. According to some sources, moving can cause situational depression, a type of temporary depression associated with moving.

The logistical preparations for a move are one factor of the stress we talk about when we discuss moving. Things like packing, arranging services in your new location, figuring out where everything will go, the act of transporting all of your items, looking for misplaced items, and other logistical issues, are one aspect of the stress. Not only can the act of moving itself be difficult, but it also requires a mindset shift as you adapt to the reality of living in a new place, or the reality of leaving a place you loved. This emotional transition that takes place adds to the tension that forms with all the logistical challenges. I think all of these types of stress have clearly been portrayed throughout this book. However, I observe that there is a deeper point of contention triggering these emotions.

I believe somewhere inside we all have a longing for home. We all long for that safe feeling. Whether it be our time spent in the womb, or that childhood feeling of being home and having magical thinking. For me I think of Grandma's house. The ice cold air conditioning on hot summer days that would wrap around my face as I walked in dripping wet from the pool. Sitting on her sofa watching TV to relax while she doted on me. Bringing me grilled cheese while simultaneously handing over the glass candy bowl that was sitting on the coffee table just barely out of the reach of my relaxed arm, which was chock full of Reese's cups, then asking if I wanted another grilled cheese. When I say "home" it is that type of home feeling that I am talking about.

Now hold that feeling and combine it with this.

Fast forward to just after childhood. The good old days of your life. The time where possibilities are endless. First loves and promiscuity. The time where backpacking through far-off lands is one hundred percent going to happen. The risk, the thrill, the absolute freedom of nothingness and the dreaming of endless adventures ahead of you. No baggage, no obligations, just you, the open road and endless possibilities.

I do not have a science to this. I do not know if there is research or relevance to this. All I have is my instincts and my lifetime of observations. And those tell me that the dichotomy of these two feelings exist in most of us. Whether it be a time in our life, a feeling in our life, or a feeling of a time in our life, we all have it deep down.

When we move, these deep instinctual feelings bubble up like a volcano. In bigger transitions they appear more severely, but with other more routine transitions, not so much. I believe that through all the chaos of a move these two feelings clash. Grandma's house—everything I could ever need along with absolute comfort—versus freedom, my way, adventure, along with the lightness of having little, with endless possibilities.

When you combine all of this with our earlier talk about the memories we attach to our things; you can see how these deep-rooted feelings could make decisions heavy. When we are debating what to keep and what to discard, feelings come up triggered by memories that leave us torn with whether to keep something or discard it. Items that hold memories of a loved one who has passed can leave us especially torn when we think of the energy said item could be taking up in our life. On the other hand items that we have no use for, that do not hold important memories, can be easily freed from our space. All of this ties into feelings that spur from the home, safe, comfort side versus the free, adventure, light side. When we move we are forced to make these decisions. The battle happens on a microcosm level with individual items and on a macro level with what we are trying to achieve with the move as a whole. Downsizing, first home, dream home, first apartment, assisted living, childhood home, college dorm, divorce house, combining houses are some of the moves that come to my mind that force tougher decisions, as opposed to more lateral moves, like moving from one apartment to another, or one office space to another.

MOVING: AN EMOTIONAL JOURNEY

Hoarding

> *"And worst of all, I would go into the most shit-filled disgust of a hoarder's house, looking human beings in the eye, terrified of how I was going to look at them, and just dole out a plan with an unjudging eye. But I never understood why until I realized almost every one of them had suffered a loss so far beyond anything I could possibly comprehend and their de facto mental response was to never let anything go again—ever!"*
>
> -Robert Esposito
>
> *Robert Esposito | Free Will, My Most Appreciated Gift | SPEAK: Freedom*

In modern society hoarding is perhaps the most extreme expression of when the emotion of things takes form.

If you're dealing with someone in your family or a friend who's experiencing a hoarding situation, consider thinking of it like an addiction. There's only so much you can do with them. It may be almost impossible for them to make a transition, remove their stuff, or clean it up. Understand what you're dealing with, and look for resources that can help such as professional organizers or therapists.

Similar to an alcoholic or a drug addict, it is easy to look down on people in your circle who have a hoarding situation. Approaching a hoarding situation, and the hoarder, with patience can go a long way. Bringing light to the situation and discussing it can sometimes lead to breakthroughs, although oftentimes that is not the case. For this discussion what is important is to understand the humanity in them, no matter the level of filth they live in. I promise no one wants to live that way. It is easy to blame the victim who causes their plight. It is harder to communicate the situation with dignity and compassion. And it is impossible for you to comprehend how someone could let such a living situation happen.

THE REAL-WORLD HACKS

1. **A moment in time.** Take pictures or video before the move to preserve memories for loved ones. You never know what circumstances may develop that will render priceless the memory of how the home looked when it was lived in.

2. **Let it go.** If you haven't touched something for years but a memory forces you to keep it close then ask yourself if it's worth the trouble of moving. Maybe take a picture? Or create a memorial piece to display using a small portion of the item. Nobody needs an item just to be in the attic for your kids to one day toss in the garbage.

3. **The why.** Clearly understand the why of the transition and the factors that contribute to this being a move you must make. When it does get tough, remember the why, and know that what you're doing is what you must do.

4. **Treat yourself right.** It's all too easy to neglect healthy eating and forego on sleep during the commotion of a move. After all, there's so much to do. But staying hydrated, getting plenty of rest, taking breaks when needed, and eating healthy will ensure you're in top-tier condition to handle the physical and emotional demands of moving.

5. **A change of scenery.** Research shows that getting out in nature has mental health benefits. Even doing something different apart from your usual routine, like taking a walk or exploring a new area, can offer a fresh perspective and re-energize you. Staring at nature does a lot for mental healing.

6. **Motion.** Motion is emotion and use this motion to help yourself start a new chapter or get on a new path. Think of all those New Year's Eve feelings.

7. **Make your new home your comfort zone.** Decorations, like wall art, candles, and photos of loved ones add a personal touch that can make your new house feel like home.

8. **Outside the family.** Do not get discouraged by friends or acquaintances when they make you feel bad for moving. People tend to pass judgment when they feel an emotion. Perhaps they are sad to see you leave; this is a kind gesture but it should not make you feel

guilty or wrong for your actions. Knowing that it is best for you and your family is always your top priority.

9. **Row together.** Discuss clearly the "why" of your transition with anyone who may be a part of the move with you. Make sure early on you are all on the same page and stay in line throughout the difficult parts of the transition.

10. **Faith like a rock.** Trust in your faith. Whether it be God, a Higher Power, the Universe, or whatever you believe in, trust that you are where you are supposed to be and doing what is a part of your plan.

THE CONCLUSION

I thought this was a book about moving? A question you may be asking yourself after reading this chapter. I get it! This is a little heavy for a book about moving. Suffice to say if you have been around enough people moving, you will agree this chapter is needed. You may even say forget all the other chapters. This chapter and the emotions that arise are the understanding you need, the technical stuff then becomes easy to figure out.

Imagine a young family splitting up a home during a divorce. The move is a personification of divorce and the tearing apart of all of the hopes and dreams of a family. Or what about that first night after you send your youngest off to college? The peace and quietness of your home that for 18 years you thought you wanted. Now suddenly the silence you once yearned for germinates into an eerie curse as you contemplate all of these empty rooms in a once bustling home. How about the move months or years after the tragic loss of a loved one? The move is the final act that cements the reality that the chapter of

MOVING: AN EMOTIONAL JOURNEY

life with that loved one has ended. Your path moves forward with circumstances different than you had ever anticipated.

By now I am sure you can conceptualize the stark difference hiring a mover may have when compared with hiring someone to build a deck or fix your roof. Most likely these last two will not strike at the core of your humanity. Other trades do not intertwine or unearth emotions because the circumstances are all different. I hope this understanding helps even if just a little.

If you're a parent and you do not understand anything I am saying here, I urge you to do this: go into your attic or basement and find something you have not seen or touched since your baby grew out of it. Maybe clothes from infancy, or perhaps your child's mattress from their crib. Smell it and you will understand the feelings.

BONUS TIP: My father always told me the only thing you can be sure of (in this world) is change itself. Making your peace with change creates the space for positive things to come to you.

> "Heraclitus, I believe, says that all things pass and nothing stays, and comparing existing things to the flow of a river, he says you could not step twice into the same river."
>
> —*Plato*

18

THE TRANSITION
PEOPLE & PLACES

"Happy and sad endings: both lead to new beginnings." —Robert Esposito

Your Heads on the Floor

Our client lived in California. He was a very nice man and we got to know him pretty well. I was a kid and I was handling a big cleanout for him. The first few days we were hosting a cleanout estate sale. The house did not have enough valuable items to host a big weekend estate sale. So instead we opted to slowly clean-out the house over the course of a couple of days, while simultaneously selling items to people that stopped by. The people came from signs we put up and advertising we had done that said we would be opening up a clean-out for people that wanted to buy some of the valuable items.

Our client appreciated this service we were willing to do and that definitely gave us a closer rapport than just client / business. I learned that he had inherited the house through his close friend. His buddy had no family and I could tell he knew he was the closest person to him. I could tell the client trusted me and on the third day he switched his flight and flew back to California. He was appreciative to leave and knew he could trust us to finish the job.

Before leaving he asked me if we rip rugs off floors and remove staples. I said "Yes" and he replied, "Great. The house has wood floors. Please remove all of them and send me the bill." A lot more work but also more money and this was a blessing for us. After the cleanout we started ripping rugs in each room. Nothing about what I have said I would ever remember. How could I? What would be the significance? We literally had been in all of these circumstances probably a thousand times.

I remember walking in the office bedroom as two of my guys had begun to pull the rug from the far side. I walked on the rug, through the room to grab the middle so the three of us could all easily rip the rug efficiently. Three people ripping a rug from one side to another is like a cold knife through warm butter. When only two people do it, a split in the rug can happen and it will slow you down. As we crossed the plane in the middle of the room I remember all three of us dropping to the floor like a wrecking ball swung through the room and leveled us all in one fell swoop. As we let go of the half pulled rug I remember seeing all three of us grab for the bottom of our t-shirts to cover our faces. A smell I had never experienced shot through my nose and throat and the taste cemented itself throughout my upper body.

We regrouped some time later and completed the job. In that room we did the best we could with shirts tied around our faces like bandanas in order to bear the smell. That night I called the client from California to review the bill and just close out the job. Bringing up what happened was kind of awkward and not my top priority because I really did not have an explanation for what had happened. I did not want to sound like I was being ridiculous by saying the rug in the office smelled really bad. Even though I do not think any of us would eat for the next couple of days. When he asked how the rest of the job went, I responded in a nonchalant manner. I said, "All went well, and I will mail out the keys. In the office we had a moment when we ripped the rug. I don't know, I am not really sure, but when we lifted the rug, a smell so bad we tasted it hit all three of us." He responded, "My God, Rob, I am so sorry. That was said to have been professionally cleaned." Quickly I thought to myself, professionally cleaned before the cleanout? That's weird. Then he said, "My buddy shot himself in that room. I was not allowed to enter until that room was approved for clearance. I am sorry. They must have done a shit job." I remained as professional as possible as we cordially hung up the phone. As I ended the call, I threw up outside my truck, as did my two workers as I yelled what the smell was. Nobody ate a thing the following day!

THE ADVICE

Maybe you're excited about moving and starting life somewhere new. At the same time, maybe you're sad about leaving all that's familiar to you in the place you've called home. As I alluded to earlier in the book, a bittersweet combination of mixed emotions surrounding a move is not really all that unusual.

Moving often involves saying goodbye to your favorite people and places. And that can be really difficult, especially if you're lucky enough to have become close with your neighbors. Remember the days when you kept special cake or drinks on hand in case your neighbors stop by, and you can serve them something good while you spend time together. Remember always hearing, "Do not touch that. I bought that in case company comes over." Those days of company seem to be long victims of technology. Neighbors on the other hand, if you're lucky, still can offer that old school feeling of community, and a special bond. Sometimes they even become like family. So when it's time to move, there can be unexpected grief as you feel their proximity beginning to slip. Give yourself that space to grieve. Even though you know you'll stay in touch—you're just a phone or video call away—you know you will no longer be able to just run next door or across the street to check in. You'll want to take time to say your goodbyes—not just to your immediate neighbors, but to the people who have been part of your community.

And then it's on to new beginnings. As you settle into your new home, you'll meet new people, and some will resonate with you right away. I'll never forget meeting one of my new neighbors and just knowing we would be close from our very first conversation. I started to say something in confidence when I first introduced myself, when I abruptly stopped because I had only just met the guy. He caught that and said "I know; we're not there yet!" I wasn't worried we instantly were there. We both laughed knowing there was nothing to worry about. We would have plenty of time for our families to get to know each other. After all, we were neighbors.

Here are some tips to help you say your goodbyes, tie up loose ends, and start your life fresh.

Your New Neighbors

Neighbors can make or break your living situation. Maybe a new neighbor will wind up being completely insignificant to you. However, a bad one can destroy your quality of life. Do not overlook the connection to neighbors and make it a top priority to start off on the right foot.

In times of distress—say, a horrific storm, a tragedy, or maybe an everyday emergency like getting your kids off the bus—a great neighbor can quickly grow into your front-line comrade. Even the person with whom you have minimal contact can wind up being the one you and your family rely on to get all of you through a zombie apocalypse.

THE REAL-WORLD HACKS

1. **Close the loop.** Take the time to say goodbye to your neighbors, but also to the people who made your life better on a regular basis—your hairdresser, manicurist, personal trainer, etc.

2. **Right away.** Make immediate introductions. This should be a quick hello with brief pleasantries.

3. **The 411.** Find similarities and use those to gather information to kick off your exploration of your new neighborhood, including the availability of kids' sports, favorite foods, the best hair salon, etc. If there is something you like about your neighbor's home, inquire so you can go directly to a trusted new vendor or service.

4. **Rolodex.** Give new neighbors your contact information and encourage them to reach out if they ever need anything.

5. **Heads up.** Take the initiative to say that if you are throwing a party or planning work on the house, you will give them plenty of advance notice.

6. **Make the necessary changes.** While you're at it, cancel your gym memberships and any other neighborhood services you pay for. Enter a change of address for any subscriptions and services you want to continue at your new home.

7. **Explore the new territory.** If possible, before the move, take a drive to your new community and explore. Which shops do you think you'll stop at the most? Where will you go for haircuts? Get to know your new community.

8. **Pack the essentials.** Confirm you have the basics you'll need for your first day in the place you now call home. A cooler packed with food and drinks can help you get through the day as you unpack. Other immediate essentials include, it's worth repeating, those heavy-duty garbage bags as well as cleaning supplies, so keep them handy.

9. **New favorites.** Research further into your new community. How will you find your new favorite places? Check out all the community and parent groups online ahead of time. And be sure to ask your new neighbors for their recommendations (more on that in the bonus tip below).

10. **First supper.** Plan dinner for your first night in the new place. Chances are, you won't be cooking that evening. Will you grab a pizza? Order in? Check online and look for the places with the best reviews.

THE CONCLUSION

At times we could all use a little help from a friend. At times we could all use a shoulder to lean on. At times we could all use a peer to debate with. At times we could all use a water cooler convo about the weather. At times we could all use a beauty parlor to gossip too.

Not really, but you get what I am saying. All of these nuances in life are what fulfills our life. My partner Tony Marisi said it best to me, "Life is lived in the moments." These people are usually the ones you capture in the moments. When your child breaks a bone. Who you're with during a 9/11 like event. When your memories freeze and the moments are emblazoned into your brain for eternity. Or just the random person you bump into for a cordial "hello" every week at the bagel store. The people and places that make up the background landscape of your life.

THE TRANSITION PEOPLE & PLACES

BONUS TIP: As you begin a relationship or acquaintance in your new community, make it a point not to sweat the small stuff when a neighbor has a request or even a complaint. By demonstrating a relaxed approach to these kinds of situations, you are modeling for them the type of approach you hope they will demonstrate in turn when you're in need or if you've created a burden.

"We can never go nowhere unless we share with each other. We gotta start makin' changes. Learn to see me as a brother instead of two distant strangers. And that's how it's supposed to be."

—Tupac Shakur, "Changes"

THE EXPERT

Bryan Karp, AKA, The Sales Giant

Founder of The Illiterate Millionaire and Mailbox Money; two-time all-American Division 1 football player

The Illiterate Millionaire / Mailbox Money

Twenty years ago, I rented a basement apartment that flooded like the Mississippi River every time it rained, with loud, barking dogs and farm animals yapping 24/7. Today, I own a real estate portfolio worth about $15 million with no debt on any of it, made up of about 20 properties and over 40 tenants. In between that, fighting cancer, and today still reading on a third or fourth grade reading level. How do you go from renting to relaxing, and collecting rent checks every month? You do it by becoming obsessed with outworking the competition. You do it by living below your means and living today like no one else, so tomorrow, you and your family could live like no one else.

After renting the basement apartment, I worked three jobs to save up a down payment to buy a legal two-family house. At that time, my beautiful wife and I were living upstairs. We rented out a two-bedroom apartment downstairs for $2,000. Our mortgage payment was $1,900. At that point, we were house-hacking and had no living expenses. From there, I mastered the game of sales and put every dollar we were blessed with back into multifamily real estate. I had the sales business doing over seven figures a year, multiple years in a row, and we were still living in a modest, three-bedroom, second-floor apartment. Today, I still drive a 2010 Camry with over 200,000 miles on it and have been financially free for over three years. That means we have more passive income coming in from our rental portfolio than we need to run and live our lives. We bought real estate when everybody was scared to. We provided a clean, safe living environment for lots of county residents; they maintain our assets. The market, as it always does, appreciated, and our wealth continued to multiply. When we were just tenants, we paid early, kept our unit spotless, and the landlord worked with us. If you put out good, good will come back to you. Over the last few years, we've been selling many of our smaller rentals and using a 1031 tax exchange into larger pieces of real estate without paying any tax.

Remember, there's nothing special about me. Anyone reading this is actually more well-equipped to build the life of their dreams.

10
WHAT MAKES YOU HAPPY?

"Let me tell you what it's all about. Find you a few things that matter, that you can put a fence around."

—From "Buy Dirt," by Jordan Davis and Luke Bryan

THE STORY

When Stamatis Moraitis was 66 years old, his doctors told him he had just six to nine months left to live.

Moraitis, who'd spent most of his adult life living in suburban New York and Florida, was getting short of breath, unable to finish a day of work like he used to. It's terminal lung cancer, his American doctors said.

So, the Greek father of three decided to move back to his homeland, on the isolated Mediterranean island of Ikaria, with his wife Elpiniki. He didn't want his family to be burdened with the thousands of dollars he knew an American funeral would cost. Let me be buried beside my family, by the sea, and where it'll only cost my relatives a few hundred dollars, he thought.

But back on Ikaria, the Greek island parked halfway between Athens and Turkey, something remarkable happened. Moraitis didn't know it at the time, but he was returning to a unique, isolated spot, an island where people routinely live past 100. He had entered a Blue Zone.

Slowly, he started to move. Breathing the fresh air, admiring the clear, blue water. Drinking wine, reconnecting with old friends. He decided to take up gardening, too.

Eventually, he started planting grapevines for a backyard vineyard. He recognized he would not be around to enjoy the wine by the time the plants were ready for harvesting, but at least his wife would have the vines as a tangible way to remember him.

Three decades later, he was still above ground, cultivating all sorts of fruits and vegetables — including grapes for wine and olives for oil — on his family's homestead, when author and longevity expert Dan Buettner visited Ikaria to learn about the island's longevity tricks.

"I asked him: what's your secret?" Buettner said, in the new Netflix docuseries *Live to 100: Secrets of the Blue Zones*. "He just kind of shrugs his shoulders and goes 'I don't know! I guess I just forgot to die.'"

We can't know for sure exactly what happened to Moraitis, precisely why he lived an additional three decades after his terminal lung cancer diagnosis. It's possible that Moraitis might have had some unique genetic qualities that so-called SuperAgers often exhibit, which can help protect them from diseases like cancer taking over.

But, Buettner suspects there is also, likely, a major component of our longevity that is not about who we are inside, but rather, what we surround ourselves with — the people, the plants, the air, the lifestyle. One oft-cited study of Danish twins suggests genetics is only responsible for about 20 to 25% of our longevity.

"He didn't do anything consciously to try to get healthier," Buettner said. "All he did was change his environment."

Buettner has even tried to re-engineer an Ikarian-like Blue Zones lifestyle in the US, with decent success. Starting in the small town of Albert Lea, Minnesota in 2009, his Blue Zones Projects work with cities to create more opportunities for people in the US to move and live like centenarians in the world's five Blue Zones do.

The projects include more opportunities for walking and exercising, improving sidewalks and building out bike lanes, as well as making healthier, plant-based meal options more accessible at grocery stores and restaurants, and providing opportunities for people to connect with their purpose, through volunteering, walking groups, gardening, or mural painting.

"I'm a big believer – if you're overweight and unhealthy in America, it's probably not your fault," Buettner, who has a new book out that is essentially a master class for adopting Blue Zones lifestyle hacks, said. "I think we're mostly victims of our environment."

For Moraitis, his environment had him climbing up a ladder to pick olives and harvest grapes up until the very end of his life.

"I'm still drinking wine and working," Moraitis told the BBC in early 2013, just a few weeks before his death, at 98 years old (or was it 102? Moraitis couldn't ever remember, exactly). "I'm no doctor, but I think the wine helped. I've done nothing else, except eat pure food, pure wine, pure herbs."

Above Story Featured on Businessinsider.com

Man With Terminal Cancer Moved to Ikaria,
Greece Blue Zone, Lived 3 Decades - Business Insider.

I first heard about Blue Zones and the story above while watching a Netflix series called *Live to 100: Secrets of the Blue Zones*. The irony! I stumbled upon the show and was immediately excited about my Sunday afternoon. I sat fascinated by these centenarians from these remote parts of the world. Communities with above average amounts of people living over 100 years old. Not only that these people were active, strong, and filled with life. Studies were revealing the factors that contribute to longevity in Blue Zones. Natural food, social community, exercise, spirituality, purpose, among some of the most important factors. The Japanese cultures were particularly interesting as they showed all the work these 100-year-old people did and how they were always kneeling and using their midsection as opposed to sitting. What a contrast as I sat on suburban Long Island on a beautiful Sunday in my extra cushioned Lazy Boy recliner. The excitement of multiple episodes of something I would enjoy faded into Sunday Sadness as I became aware of the irony of my current predicament. Noted, modern society has got this all wrong!

THE ADVICE

If you think I am about to preach to you about how you need to change your life and live in a natural or experimental Blue Zone, well then you're very wrong. Telling anyone how they should live their life is the antithesis of anything I would ever stand for. This story's purpose is to give you a glimpse into a way of life that exists out there. After all, how could I write a book about moving and not at least allude to the fact that there are places and lifestyles you could choose that remarkably contribute to living a long active quality of life? We all understand that where we move has a dramatic impact on the way of life we live. However, when we move, I do not think we give much weight to the impact our location has on our actual life expectancy. "Cent'anni" (which is an Italian toast that signifies health and happiness for 100 years)!

Views from the Mover

As a mover, I've learned a lot, including getting to know every town in the metropolitan New York City area. I know every block, every 7-Eleven, every gas station, every great food spot, every everything I may need wherever I am. With this kind of incidental knowledge, I became very specific about where I choose to live. Being in so many neighborhoods, so many different homes, and seeing so many different types of lifestyles up close, has given me a unique perspective on lifestyle and housing choices. I tend to analyze areas when I travel differently than someone that is not in this field of work. Often on vacation, when I take a car service from an airport to my hotel in a foreign country, I catch myself daydreaming about what it would be like to live in the houses I pass. When it comes to how people live, being in this field has given me two gifts that I appreciate. It has given me the gift of seeing more than most, and paying attention or noticing the little things more than most.

Below in the Hacks section I switched things up a little. The following section is less of a how to section and more geared towards personal choices. Things to get you thinking in hopes it will lead to you making choices that suit you and your family's needs and wants.

THE REAL WORLD HACKS

Personally, I like ranches. I like larger property. I like being close to highways and shopping, and central locations where I can get to a lot of different places in 30 minutes or less. For now, I prefer this kind of location rather than a beach town, coastal area, or rural mountain area, where the people tend not to leave as much. I know that people's needs and circumstances change. I'm sure that in time, mine will too. Knowing what type of conditions best suit your current lifestyle is key to choosing the right home for you.

Set Up Your Home for How You Want to Live

From my work, I know that each home and each client needs support in any number of ways and I always step up to see how I can help. I've come across every kind of living situation, from spending time in the homes of type-A, super-organized personalities to those with total disregard for their home's appearance—and everything in between. I've long admired homes with rooms that no one can go in. White rugs with forever-fresh vacuum marks. I never understood the museum rooms but I appreciate them and I'm sure they're there to be admired.

Our home is our safe zone, the place we go to relax and decompress. Some believe it's a sacred space, as it's the place that holds some of our most important memories and experiences. The term *feng shui* translates to "the way of wind and water," which emphasizes the natural flow of our lives.

Your personality type and the needs of you and your family can also inform how you set up your home. Young families will benefit from a different layout than busy professionals or those who are retired or single. Intentionally setting up your home based on your lifestyle can maximize your comfort in your new home. Even if you're moving into a small space with limited options for furniture arrangements, the way you arrange your belongings can mean the difference between being able to relax at the end of the day…or not. Keeping walkways clear so that you don't have to navigate around furniture or other objects, along with decluttering, can bring a sense of peace and calm to your environment. Incidentally, the aforementioned are also feng shui principles.

The Right House at the Right Time

People often ask me which is the best area and the ideal setup to live comfortably on Long Island. The answer? It depends on the individual. Parents of young kids who are in the market for a house might consider buying a home in neighborhoods with one-acre lots and ranch houses. As a mover, I've come to love these kinds of sprawling ranch homes. Because they are all one-story, they eliminate the need to go up and down stairs. Maybe years of moving furniture up and down stairs has caused me to be biased.

Now, I might feel differently if I lived by the water. There, a house with stairs would bring another dimension, including views and idyllic perspectives to see the sun rise or set. But that's the only thing I would sacrifice for in the future. If I were downsizing, I might consider moving close to the water, into a house with multiple levels so I could enjoy the views.

Treasure relationships, not things. Construct your home to build memories.

In every house I've ever lived in, I've put a pool table in my living room. I love playing pool. Both as a kid and as a mover, I've noticed that people usually put the pool table in the basement and never use it. My wife and I play at least two nights a week, especially on weekends. After the kids go to bed, we enjoy drinks, play music, and shoot pool. The pool table is the first thing you see when you walk into my house, and anyone who stops by winds up shooting a game of pool and talking.

My living room is wide open and connects with the kitchen. I love wide-open houses, where the central living area has few walls. Ideally, the master bedroom is on the other side of the house, separated from the children's rooms by all the common areas, so everyone has their space. And, when it comes to practicality, I have a theory that one of the biggest misconceptions in American culture is that, because refrigerators come with ice makers, you'll always have enough ice, but you inevitably end up needing more ice than the refrigerator can provide every time you have people over. All houses should just come with an ice machine! Rarely does someone with a stove not also have a microwave and toaster oven. Why because refrigerators make ice do we forgo also having small ice machines? Maybe I am being ridiculous but it always seems to be a point of contention when having people over.

When I was just starting out and had very little, I used to marvel at the people I would move who had money. I wasn't marveling about what they had. Instead, I was fascinated by the concept that most of them constructed inviting homes so people would always want to come over. I was intrigued by those who created homes that encouraged their grown children to stay as long as possible.

These houses often had a movie room with posters, popcorn machines, and even concession items. There would sometimes be an arcade with ping pong tables and maybe even a bowling lane. The homes were warm and inviting. The garages were filled with go carts, dune buggies, skis, motorcycles, and other fun, off-road vehicles. The yards were huge with a tremendous pool. There would be speakers everywhere. And right next to the pool would be a pergola with a TV and a fan, firepit, and outdoor sofa, a place where the parents in the neighborhood would watch baseball games on warm summer nights while having a cocktail as the kids play next to them in the pool. Some of the houses had a separate grandparents' wing for aging parents that could double as an apartment for a young adult child. It's a home that would have been next to impossible for children to move out of in haste when they were old enough to. Although I also saw the entitled, spoiled, negative side of this choice, I choose not to focus on that and instead reach for the ideal.

The ability to have that type of success and to create that type of environment is without a doubt a dream by most measures. The picture drawn from success above is just one side of the personification of these ideals. Home is a feeling and you do not have to have any type of great success to achieve any of these ideals. Closeness, warmth, belonging, security, comfort, love, are all feelings we attribute to a happy home. None of which in a home require more than the most basic level of success to achieve.

THE CONCLUSION

As I pointed out in the beginning of this book, if you Google "life's biggest stressors," the results list death, divorce, moving, and serious illness—in that order. But moving is a trade. How does it come before cancer? Strangers come and take all of your stuff. But things are just objects; objects mean nothing. It's the memories we attach to those things that mean everything.

> *"The truth about it is, it all goes by real quick. You can't buy happiness, but you can buy dirt."*
>
> —*From "Buy Dirt," by Jordan Davis and Luke Bryan*

Our relationships, not our objects, are what is most important. I wish for your home to be a place of comfort and solace, where you will be surrounded by the people and things that hold your memories, that carry you through a lifetime of memories. Enjoy your journey, and your new beginning.

The Conclusion of the 1st Act

ABOUT THE AUTHOR

"Study harder the people you do not want to be like than the people you do want to be like. Knowing what not to do is as crucial as knowing what to do. And always trust your gut"

—*Robert Esposito*

In his 17 years in the moving business, and some 50,000 moves across the United States, Robert Esposito has seen his share of personal sagas. The downsizing. The upgrading. The need to pack up after a breakup or to clean out a home because a loved one has passed.

What's emerged for Robert is not only a solid business venture, but also the opportunity to have a close-up look at the human condition, the vulnerability of risk-taking at the intersection of free will and fate. Over time, Robert has transformed into an entrepreneur, as well as an everyday philosopher, taking pride in helping people move through life's transitions, no matter how challenging. Robert often jokes, "Understanding people's nature is both frustrating and a curse. I have trouble getting mad at people at times when I should, because I understand their why."

Excerpt from Speak Podcast - Fred Banny - The Builder

That was Rob Esposito with his talk "Free Will, My Most Appreciated Gift." Now Rob is someone who I like to refer to as an everyday philosopher. What Rob does in his everyday work I think gives him a depth of human experience because he has the opportunity to work with people during the most vulnerable moments and that's when our real true nature comes out. I think because of that he has seen people in different stages and phases in different scenarios and this has caused him to just reflect and contemplate on the meaning of life, right? And those are deep things that we sometimes shy away from. So Rob's talk was really a joy to listen to, and even working with him was a joy. He's unpretentious, but then when he opens his mouth you see this is a philosopher, an "everyday philosopher" I like to call him, so Rob, thank you for stepping up into the spotlight onto the stage to deliver your talk.

Excerpt from Speak Podcast - George Andriopoulos - The Architect

Welcome to another episode of the Speak podcast. I'm your host for today, George Andreopoulos, The Architect and one of the co-leaders here at Speak. Our first talk for this episode comes from published speaker Rob Esposito. While weaving in and out of both professional and personal stories, Rob Esposito gives us an in-depth look into the freedom of the will and the power of choice. He uses real life experiences to display how finding perspective and taking risks can remove the lie that society tells us, which is that at a certain point in our lives we lose control of our lives and become controlled by Fate. Now this talk was so much fun to work with, with Rob. When Rob came to us for our freedom event in July of 2023 he had so much to say, and I remember working with him and seeing his first draft and realizing that this guy was not only an incredible entrepreneur and business owner but he was a poet of sorts, and he was just incredibly deep in some of the thoughts that he put forth in this talk. His story of perseverance was just so amazing, and to hear his perspective on the work that he does with his company Relocators was just amazing. That's all I can say about it. o without any further ado, here's Rob Esposito with "Free Will, My Most Appreciated Gift."

George Andriopoulos
"The Architect"/Co-Leader at SPEAK

Fred P. Banny III

"The Builder"/Co-Leader at SPEAK

www.speakevent.com

"As a global public speaking platform that seeks to amplify voices across the world, SPEAK was delighted to have Rob Esposito on our stage because he did the exact thing that we look for out of the stories on our stage. He humanized some of the subject matter of his talk, which happened to be about the act of moving, and through the story he helped the audience understand that moving was just as much an emotional journey as it is a physical journey."

Robert Esposito | Free Will, My Most Appreciated Gift | SPEAK: Freedom

A Note from Robert

From my earliest memory, I had a deep interest in understanding why people do what they do. I was always analyzing people's behavior and actions. Throughout my experiences, I have adapted this analysis through different perspectives based on what stage of life I was in, as well as what stage of life the other person is in. My bachelor's degree is in Human Relations, which prepared me with an understanding of psychology and sociology. I also spent a lot of time studying acting and theology. Prior to starting my company, my only real job was in the restaurant business. There, too, I learned to read people's behaviors. Examples include the apathy you can see in a couple who are bored with their relationship, or the joy of a family who saved up all month for their one special night at a restaurant. There are tell-tale patterns in human communication, both verbal and nonverbal. Nowhere is this more noticeable than during an extremely stressful transition, such as moving, and it becomes even more pronounced when coupled with a death or divorce. My hope is for people to understand that, although they are unique and precious, their experiences and circumstances are often routine. We all go through things and the stages of life that cause dramatic transitions are just part of life's routines, which we all must face—if we are so lucky.

Tragically, I had one of my closest friends pass at the age of 18. Years later, my wife, who had never met him, visited a psychic. She returned and said that my friend requested that I ask his mom to remove the shirt from her bed. This confused me, but I made sense of it because I had the bloody shirt I wore the night he passed, along with some of my dad's FDNY clothes in a bag under my bed. I registered it and then I let it go. I tried not to think too deeply about the psychic part.

Years later, I moved his mom out of state. My guys lifted the mattress and I found out my friend's high school football jersey was pressed between the mattresses. The important part of the story is this.

I did not need a psychic, nor did I need it to be my best friend's mom's mattress, to know that the jersey was not just any jersey; it was a stored memory of a very important event—one that had transformed this woman's life. In the end, it's not our things that are important. Our things are just things; the memories we place on them are what give them value.

The Author's Favorite Poem
Desiderata

Go placidly amid the noise and the haste, and remember what peace there may be in silence. As far as possible, without surrender, be on good terms with all persons.

Speak your truth quietly and clearly; and listen to others, even to the dull and the ignorant; they too have their story.

Avoid loud and aggressive persons; they are vexatious to the spirit.

If you compare yourself with others, you may become vain or bitter, for always there will be greater and lesser persons than yourself.

Enjoy your achievements as well as your plans. Keep interested in your own career, however humble; it is a real possession in the changing fortunes of time.

Exercise caution in your business affairs, for the world is full of trickery. But let not this blind you to what virtue there is; many persons strive for high ideals, and everywhere life is full of heroism.

Be yourself. Especially do not feign affection. Neither be cynical about love; for in the face of all aridity and disenchantment, it is as perennial as the grass.

Take kindly the counsel of the years, gracefully surrendering the things of youth.

Nurture strength of spirit to shield you in sudden misfortune. But do not distress yourself with dark imaginings. Many fears are born of fatigue and loneliness.

Beyond a wholesome discipline, be gentle with yourself. You are a child of the universe no less than the trees and the stars; you have a right to be here.

And whether or not it is clear to you, no doubt the universe is unfolding as it should.

Therefore, be at peace with God, whatever you conceive Him to be. And whatever your labors and aspirations, in the noisy confusion of life, keep peace in your soul. With all its sham, drudgery and broken dreams, it is still a beautiful world. Be cheerful.

Strive to be happy.

—by Max Ehrmann, 1927

The Experts

Ron Starrantino - Real Estate Pro / dedicated page on real estate

Randy Goldbaum - Egress Pros

Matt Rivera - Inspection Boys' founder

Bryan Karp - Renter Tips/Cash Home Buyer (biggest cash homebuyer in New York)

Steven Pike - Assisted living director who own major home health aide business

Andrew Lamkin - Estate Attorney

James Garvey - Loan Officer

Steven Shumer - Divorce Attorney

Dan Kluger - Restoration Moves

Nicolas Castillo - Bright! Tax; International Moves

Mike Scaialabba - Military Moves

Andy Hanellin - Pets

Jeanine Gagliano - (Estate sales) Right at Home South Shore Long Island

Sandi Polinsky - (Estate Sales)

The Celebrities with Experience

Lee Zeldin - Military Moves

Zeldon Hamilton - (Former NY Knick)

Snooki - Business Moves (Her Store)

Dee Snider - Horror Story Prologue

The Thank You's

Thank you to everyone above for supporting me in helping those who are embarking on their transition out of a home and into a new one—an event that is one of the most stressful endeavors anyone will have to do in life.

A special thank-you to:

Cynthia Constantino for accepting an edit after 14 denials by editors on the self-published book, which led to assistance with ghostwriting once the book was picked up.

Robert Mayer for all of your memes and illustrations. I appreciate you everyday stopping what you're doing to bring all of my crazy whims, and visions, to life.

Stephanie Larkin of Red Penguin Books for taking the chance on Ron's recommendation and believing in what we were doing.

Ron Starrantino, a dear friend I planned a random lunch with, strictly because we missed each other. That friendly lunch took what was supposed to be a simple, self-published, competitive tool for a company based in New York City and enabled it to be offered to the masses.

Ron Starrantino
- Award Winning Real Estate Agent
- Celebrity Manager / Agent

A Personal Note from Ron Starrantino-

My favorite part about being a top real estate agent on Long Island is setting a new standard for the real estate experience I curate for my clients. Transparency, communication, & dedication are the foundations I build on. As someone fully immersed in real estate – the only thing constant in this market is change.

In my role as a top real estate agent on Long Island, my approach is not just about transactions but about transforming experiences. I am dedicated to delivering personalized, exceptional client experiences that resonate long after the deal is done.

With a profound knowledge of the Long Island housing market, specifically honed in to Nassau & Suffolk Counties, I offer more than just guidance—I offer strategic insights that are pivotal in navigating complex negotiations with confidence and clarity.

However, what truly distinguishes me is my unwavering commitment to personalized service. I don't just listen to my clients; I immerse myself in their aspirations and objectives. By understanding their unique needs and goals, I ensure that every buying or selling journey is crafted to meet their exact requirements.

Transparency is at the core of my practice. I empower my clients with comprehensive information and honest advice, enabling them to make informed decisions with confidence. This transparency builds trust and fosters a collaborative relationship, essential for achieving successful outcomes in real estate transactions.

My story is not just about numbers and listings but about the people I serve and the profound impact of tailored service in real estate. It's about setting a new standard—one where dedication, insight, and transparency redefine what it means to excel in this industry.

My Advice -

I always remember that I am not just selling a house, but that I am selling a home. I remind my clients, once we go into contract, that 'home is where your heart is.' I suggest starting by hanging pictures in the home to create that warm, familiar feeling and set the mood for nesting and settling in."

The Epilogue

"In Life as well as in Moving: take ACCOUNT for what you are ABLE to see is your responsibility"
—Robert Esposito

That damn fickle finger, Again

One time we were moving someone who was celebrity-connected to North Carolina. This client was a well-respected veteran as well as just a great all-around human being. He was also a philanthropist. He came as a personal business referral and from the first contact I had a great rapport with him.

We hired a really reputable trucking company to transport his belongings. On all long-distance moves, we either fly out our foreman and hire local labor, or send our drivers in our trucks and have them hire local labor. The client had a tractor trailer's worth of stuff and I really wanted the move to be as smooth as possible. I decided to rent a tractor because we did not have one and I figured that would be the easiest means of transporting all his items.

We spent two days loading his belongings and expected him two days later in North Carolina. On the first day, out of nowhere the broker called me and said he could not get a hold of his driver. He basically was telling me he had zero answers. How could this be? How is this happening again? Remembering the "Reno" event in my earlier years. This time I had less answers, less control, and a much deeper connection to the client.

THE EPILOGUE

I will never forget being on a Saturday dinner date with my wife and spending the entire time on the phone with the client. The client was a wonderful guy, and it was the most terrible feeling that I had to break the news to him that I did not have any answers. Not having those answers, having the guy's life on the truck, and knowing how great of a person he was made the situation all the more surreal. He treated me so well and I wanted so badly to do an amazing job for him and his family. Throughout our convos he stayed so cool and was looking out for me more than I was looking out for him.

He knew this entire job was now going to be trouble for me. He also knew I was going to spend a lot of money to do the job and he knew no matter what I would do the right thing. His faith in me never wavered and I appreciated that. To make matters worse I had sent my foreman and top laborer down and they were awaiting the unloading, at a nearby hotel. When I told my forman he hit me with some news that just ended the whole situation for me. He said, oh shit; tomorrow is his 50th Birthday. The guy's 50th Birthday was the day we were supposed to move him into his new home. I instructed my foreman to deliver a bottle of champagne and food courtesy of all of us. It was an appreciated gesture that hardly sufficed.

The next day the freight company got a hold of the driver and the items were delivered one day late. In the end, we got everything back. There was a little damage, because it was probably handled incorrectly and everything was shaken in the truck wherever the driver vanished to. But we transported his belongings and he was happy when we were accountable and rectified any of the issues.

THE CONCLUSION

Fate.

Ron Starrantino, from the "Thank You's" section, is someone I have known for years from business networking, and has become a close personal friend of mine. Ron and I had not seen each other in years, so we went out to lunch while I was writing a book. A book, not this book, but a book like this book. A smaller self-published book I planned to use to help my clients to better prepare them for moving.

During our four hour lunch Ron and I discussed absolutely everything, including a few minutes where I told him about my idea for a helping "how to" book, that I was a few weeks away from self-publishing. Ron is a top real estate agent on Long Island. He also is Dee Snider's manager and close friend. Ron has worked in Hollywood extensively over the years. The day following our lunch I got a call from Ron. He said, "I hope you don't mind. I explained your book to a publisher I know and she would like to meet you." This lunch led to the publishing of this book. But wait!

Five years prior to the lunch meeting, it was Ron who referred me to one of his best friends. That best friend Ron referred me to is named Mike. The same client Mike, I talk about in the above story you just read about.

About a month into writing this book, which was about a month after Ron and my lunch meeting, I received a surprising phone call. It was Dee Snider himself asking me to move him and his family from Los Angeles to North Carolina. Dee had been referred to me by Rrr. Rrr. Rrrrrr. NOT Ron! Instead he was referred to me by his buddy, Mike. Mike, whom I had not spoken to in years. Mike, whom I caused that terrible experience with on his 50th Birthday. The same Mike in

THE EPILOGUE

the story above referred his close celebrity friend Dee Snider to entrust me to move his family across the entire country.

Over the next week or so Dee and I had spoken a number of times. I told him about my book and asked him if he was willing to write a feature. I had features from various experts, and celebrities we had moved in the past. Being that Dee was an author himself, it made perfect sense for me to ask him. Upon receiving Dee's feature I was so appreciative and blown away by the story Dee wrote that I added the prologue specifically for him. His story was the perfect story as it encompassed exactly my motivation for writing the book. My plan was to ask him to write a follow up after the move with my company. Once I knew he had an incredible experience I would use that story as an epilogue.

I also planned on asking Mike to give me a feature for the tenth chapter on military moves. Lee Zeldin and Mike were going to be my features for military moves. Now at this time I knew Mike's horror story about losing his truck on his 50th birthday was going to be a story in the book. Then I received Mike's expert feature about military moves.

Yes, that is right, the horror story in the tenth chapter about a lifetime of military moves gone wrong is Mike's personal story!

So I found out from Mike's feature for my book that this hero had spent a lifetime having the government absolutely destroy every move he had ever made. Then to make it even worse, I now realized that years later I would go on to destroy his 50th birthday and put him in the exact situation of having all his items missing during a move. Never once during the turmoil of his move with me did Mike say a word about his past experiences. He did not put his past on me or even bring it up. As I sit here writing this, my company has recently completed Dee's family's move. After connecting all these dots I realized the real life events are a much better epilogue.

A decade after the Reno fiasco with the lost out-of-state tractor, came Mike's out-of-state tractor job. I did everything in my power to make sure Mike's out-of-state tractor job was seamless. Sometime's things happen and they are out of your control. Extenuating circumstances exist in all areas of business as they do in life. At the moment while something is happening it always feels monumental. Was Mike's move a failure? A half a century ago Dee Snider's dad had a monumental experience. The way that experience was handled led to a man, who rarely cursed, to spend the rest of his days reflexively giving the middle finger. As for Mike, Mike was the first person on Facebook to congratulate me when my company posted about purchasing our first tractor trailer.

Then some time later he referred me to a Rockstar!

I am not going to ask Dee to write me a follow-up feature. Rather I will just tell you to trust me. If Dee wrote another story I guarantee this story would be way different than the story he wrote for the prologue. You could bet your fickle finger on it!

Accountability. It is all about accountability; in life, as well as in moving. That is what you need to look for and hire!

The End

www.ingramcontent.com/pod-product-compliance
Lightning Source LLC
Chambersburg PA
CBHW061733070526
44585CB00024B/2652